C00 44019025

EDINB D0269434

.ARIES

.te shown.
·ber.

CYRILLE REGIS
MY STORY

First published in 2010 by

André Deutsch
an imprint of the
Carlton Publishing Group
20 Mortimer Street
London W1T 3JW

Text copyright © Cyrille Regis/Chris Green 2010
Design copyright © Carlton Books Limited 2010

All rights reserved. No part of this publication may be reproduced,
stored in a retrieval system, or transmitted in any form or by any means,
electronic, mechanical, photocopying, recording or otherwise, without
the prior permission of the copyright owner and the publishers.

A CIP catalogue record for this book is available from the British
Library

ISBN: 978 0 233 00311 5

The publishers would like to thank the following sources for their kind
permission to reproduce the pictures in this book:

Section 1: Page 1: Cyrille Regis (top & bottom). Page 2: Cyrille Regis
(top & bottom). Page 3: Cyrille Regis (top), Colorsport (bottom). Page
4: Colorsport. Page 5: Mirrorpix (top & bottom). Page 6: Cyrille Regis
(top), Mirrorpix (bottom). Page 7: S&G and Barratts/Press Association
Images. Page 8: Colorsport (top), Cyrille Regis (bottom). Section 2: Page
1: Bob Thomas/Getty Images (top), Peter Robinson/Press Association
Images (middle), S&G and Barratts/Press Association Images (bottom).
Page 2: Bob Thomas/Getty Images (top), Peter Robinson/Press
Association Images (bottom). Page 3: Bob Thomas/Getty Images.
Page 4: Action Images (top), David Edsam/Alamy (bottom). Page 5:
Clive Brunskill/Getty Images (top), Cyrille Regis (bottom). Page 6:
Tim Easthope/Birmingham Post & Mail (top), Michael Steele/Press
Association (bottom). Page 7: British Ceremonial Arts Ltd (top), Cyrille
Regis (bottom). Page 8: Cyrille Regis (top, middle & bottom).

Every effort has been made to acknowledge correctly and contact the
source and/or copyright holder of each picture and Carlton Books
Limited apologises for any unintentional errors or omissions that will be
corrected in future editions.

Printed in Great Britain

CYRILLE REGIS

MY STORY

THE AUTOBIOGRAPHY OF THE FIRST
BLACK ICON OF BRITISH FOOTBALL

As told to Chris Green

ANDRE
DEUTSCH

This book is dedicated in memory of my parents, Robert and Mathilda Regis. I can never thank you enough for the love and encouragement you gave me throughout my life. I miss you dearly and will be eternally grateful to you both.

EDINBURGH LIBRARIES	
C0044019025	
Bertrams	08/09/2010
	£18.99
PR	GV942.7

Contents

Foreword

by David James

I would like to thank Cyrille for two things. Firstly, for the opportunity to add the foreword to this enlightening book. Secondly, and more profoundly, for giving me a sense of how his achievements, unknown to him, impacted on my own career.

I took my own first steps in the game at the age of nine. My school friends Daniel Novelli and Stephen James would invite me to play for their Sunday League team, Welwyn Pegasus. We spent hours playing on the fields by Dan's house in Welwyn Garden City or in his front room or hallway. This is common behaviour among school kids up and down the country, but my friends were West Bromwich Albion fans, and this was my introduction to Cyrille Regis.

Dan would draw pictures of Cyrille scoring goals. His images, true to the real life man mountain, showed the physique of an ancient Roman gladiator. Given the fact that my friends were white English schoolchildren, the admiration of Cyrille could have been surprising when you consider the social issues of the late 1970s and early 1980s. Race played no part in this at the time. I didn't think of myself as being black, or about the significance of emerging black footballers (whether they were British or not). We were just three kids enjoying our football and having a hero in the form of Cyrille Regis.

The experience for Cyrille was different, of course. It is remarkable to read about Cyrille's battles with racism, both on and off the field. Had not black players like him and a few others fought for the right to play football in such harsh conditions the door would not have been open for the likes of myself, Rio Ferdinand, John Barnes and many other gifted (and some not so gifted!) players of ethnic origin.

I am so grateful to Cyrille and his fellow trailblazers for helping to bring about racial equality in English football and for the fact that I can write these words while with the England squad, during the 2010 World Cup finals in South Africa. Thank you.

This book reveals what is going through your mind when you are trying to make it as a footballer. Although Cyrille came through the school of hard knocks, there's no doubt that, to the people around him, he is always destined to be someone special. There are parallels between Cyrille's early career and my own in this respect – the uncertainty of what the game is about and what you are going to achieve.

We both come from large families. Cyrille has seven brothers and sisters and I am one of eight, with three half-brothers and sisters. Unfortunately my family relationships are more distant than Cyrille's. Also we both had remarkable managers and coaches who helped us reach extraordinary heights in our profession.

Cyrille is a legend, and his continued work within football is highly valued. Quite simply, he is a gentleman who has helped the beautiful game become the world's game.

David James
Rustenburg, 25 June 2010

Preface

by Chris Green

If you're going to have heroes, have great ones. Generally heroes turn out to be a disappointment. They are rarely the people they seem or that we want them to be. Why should they be? Too often fans put heroes on unbelievably high pedestals.

Cyrille Regis stands apart. He remains my hero. In my youth, as a West Bromwich Albion fan, I was intoxicated by his exciting style of football and the many fantastic goals he scored for the team I supported. I was privileged to see his debut matches in the League Cup, the Football League and the FA Cup. Typically for Cyrille, he scored in each of them.

But I was soon more mightily impressed by the immense dignity with which Cyrille, as a young man in his teens and early 20s, and his team-mates Laurie Cunningham and Brendon Batson – who were dubbed West Brom's "Three Degrees" – handled the unprecedented racist abuse hurled at them. Indeed I was impressed by all the pioneering black British footballers of their generation who smashed through that particular glass ceiling.

For this reason alone Cyrille was an important footballer. Those emerging black players shouldn't have been subjected to the taunts they were forced to endure – indeed English football would have been in a far healthier state if football's timid authorities at the time had been proactive in banishing the perpetrators from their midst.

So Cyrille had an effect on me as a young man – socially and even politically rather than merely as a sportsman. It would take subsequent generations of black footballers to put this into a more defined context. Their testimonies of drawing direct inspiration from Cyrille turn ideology into reality. The Three Degrees made a palpable difference.

From slightly further afield, I recall watching with enormous delight Cyrille collecting his long-deserved FA Cup winners' medal with Coventry City and his late-career flourish at Aston Villa and Wolves.

I have also had the privilege to work with Cyrille on a few charitable projects involving Midlands youth football and on a number of media programmes I have made to which he has contributed. It isn't without good reason that Cyrille is highly regarded and fondly remembered among journalists and the general public as one of football's good guys.

On our way to a meeting at Villa Park a fan literally bumped into Cyrille. He was simply gobsmacked and, when he found himself staring at him face to face, could only utter the word "legend". If pressed for one word to describe Cyrille, that would be my choice too. Legend.

Sometimes I've had to pinch myself to take in the fact that, out of all the journalists in the world who might have helped Cyrille write his autobiography, the opportunity has fallen to me.

Cyrille, or course, offered more than inspiration. He scored spectacular goals. He thrilled crowds. When I talk to fellow supporters of other clubs they will often comment on a special goal they saw Cyrille score. Few of his goals seemed to be tap-ins – most of them had an air of quality.

He is often described as a good guy and a role model. While this is undoubtedly true, and a complimentary characteristic anyone would wish to have, it is nonetheless a rather shallow description of a man with a far deeper personality which is revealed perhaps for the first time in this autobiography.

Some of the personal details peeled open in this book may take some of the sheen off Cyrille's public image. He has been brave to lay bare the honest realities of a more complicated character.

Although much of this book is a happy wander down football's memory lane, opening up completely has not been easy for Cyrille. He has chosen to write this book – partly to inspire, partly to put things on record, but mainly to show you that anyone can turn their life around when they have made mistakes that have impacted on those around them.

Now in his early 50s, unlike many ex-footballers, who really do struggle to know what to do and how to fill their time, Cyrille is at a stage in his life where he is content. Bless him, he is also truly happy. He has an unshakeable religious faith. There is depth to his conviction.

It has been a refreshing joy and an immense privilege to hear Cyrille recall the details of his remarkable life. It is also a relief to see how the brash, bustling, streetwise centre-forward who thrilled crowds and filled grounds in his youth has matured into a warm, intelligent person who is able to articulate the many and varied things that have happened to him through a distinguished career. Frankly, many sportsmen lack that ability.

I believe he is a legend – and that he will be all the more admirable to readers of his autobiography.

Preface

I'd like to thank all the people who have helped me during the writing of this book: Cyrille and his wife Julia, Cyrille's sister Nilla, Cyrille's former sports teacher Ken Ward, Brendon Batson, John Sillett, Derek Statham, Ricky Hill, Bobby Ross (former manager) and Alan Carrington (former player) of Hayes FC and John Sullivan – the former chairman/manager of Molesey FC. David Harrison also supplied valuable nuggets of information.

Many thanks to representatives from Hayes & Yeading FC, West Bromwich Albion, Coventry City, Wolverhampton Wanderers, Molesey and Wycombe Wanderers for supplying Cyrille's appearance and goalscoring records.

Thanks also to my literary agent Robert Dudley and especially to my wife, Teresa, the fastest sub-editor in the West (Midlands), who has offered her usual unstinting love and support.

Chris Green
Author and broadcaster
Worcester, April 2010

Acknowledgements

by Cyrille Regis, MBE

Most footballers tend to write their autobiographies either during their career or shortly afterwards. I have chosen to write mine in my early 50s, some 15 years after hanging up my boots.

Why now? Partly, I guess, because I have reached an appropriate time to reflect on my life. In 2008, at the age of 50, I was awarded an MBE for services to charity and to football. Somehow the timing seems right. Also, when you are in the maelstrom of a career there is little time to pause for clarity of thought or to predict, with any degree of accuracy or perspective, how things might pan out in future.

Partly it is because of the level of interest, even now, in the early part of my career, as a pioneering black British footballer who was one of a number of players who helped transform elite football. Mainly, though, I want to tell my story.

The legend of my football career can be condensed into a few simple facts. I was spotted on Regent's Park, signed by two non-League clubs, first Molesey, then Hayes, sold to First Division West Bromwich Albion, scoring on my debut and becoming one of Albion's all-time heroes. I was an England centre-forward, an FA Cup-winning medallist with Coventry City, and had a late playing career resurgence at Villa and Wolves.

Yet this book is about my entire life. It's not just the story of my playing career, or a précis of great games and great goals. It covers my life before I became a professional footballer, what has happened after I hung up my boots, and a lot of detail beneath the headlines in between. Football has been central to my life, but it has not been my entire existence and certainly isn't the be-all and end-all for me.

I have decided to share with you the aspects of my character and behaviour that I am not so proud of. Not because I am still in need of forgiveness, or in a low place, or want to embellish my story to sell more copies, but because I know that transparency and openness about my mistakes as well as my successes might help others. I am constantly asked

Acknowledgements

to share my story up and down the country. Many, many people have said to me, Cyrille, you need to write your book and let everyone know your story. I agree with them and now feel it is the time to do so.

My intention is to give you an honest picture of my life and to let you know a little more about my life experience – the enticing intoxication of fame, wealth and free time that are part of the rush of life in a top-flight football career. There are also the dark days, and having to dig myself out of a mid-career hole when I lost my touch and some of my self-respect as a footballer.

I do not believe I am a particularly remarkable person. I may have been given a unique sporting talent which I used well. Well enough, though? Maybe not. I believe I only ever achieved two-thirds of my potential.

This book goes beyond the 90 minutes. Writing it hasn't been easy – but has proved a cathartic experience. Sitting down to discuss my life with author and broadcaster Chris Green has raised all kinds of emotions. Chris is a non-judgemental type of guy. As a vastly experienced journalist, I know he has interviewed all types of people who have endured all kinds of personal events and disasters. Chris is also a West Brom fan who watched my first ever match for the Baggies – and as a teenager travelled the length and breadth of England watching my early career unfold.

In fact, I have written this book during a time when I have found happiness and contentment in my life. This would not have been possible without God. Becoming a born-again Christian was undoubtedly the most important decision of my life – and the best.

As for thanking people who have helped shape my life, there have been so many. Most of them I have referred to in my book. I thank all the people I have mentioned from the bottom of my heart. I am grateful to you all.

Most of all, I thank God for always being with me, never leaving me, loving me unconditionally and changing my life around. I dare not think where I might be if I had not turned to God's righteous path. When you have read this book maybe you will realize why.

Cyrille Regis, MBE
Birmingham
April, 2010

CYRILLE REGIS
MY STORY

CHAPTER ONE

A Quiet Moment of Reflection

Champagne, steam, cheers, shouts, songs, hugs, wet towels, suits, deodorant and aftershave. Men are embracing each other in sheer delight at their combined achievements. It is all happening around me. Mayhem – and rightly so.

This is the dressing-room at Wembley Stadium at 5.40pm on Saturday, 16 May 1987, and Coventry City have just lifted the FA Cup following a 3–2 win over Tottenham Hotspur after extra time.

Me? I'm sitting down and staring at my winners' medal, enjoying a quiet moment of contemplation. This is my first ever medal in 10 years as a professional footballer and I am savouring the moment. It is a quiet moment. For me, the drinking will start later. Big time. First, though, I feel an overwhelming need to reflect.

I ponder the dark days of previous seasons when it seemed my career was disappearing down the chute. I reflect on the character I have shown to come back. Everything I'd gone through to claw my way back from the wilderness. The seemingly bad decision I had made to join Coventry from West Brom in 1984. I should have left Albion earlier when I was in form – not during a lean spell. I had few options. We all learn from our mistakes. I had nearly paid an enormous price.

I had proven to have the courage and confidence in myself to come through the dark days and nights of soul-searching and the desperation of seeking solace in drink and adulterous relationships. I had been on the verge of self-destruction – but had reined myself back in.

Fortitude, determination, hunger, drive, the winning mentality – I had shown all of these essential characteristics. These are attributes that don't reveal themselves when you are doing well and life seems on the up and up. When you're struggling is when you find out who you really are.

At times I did not know who the real Cyrille Regis was. In time, I would have to be literally reborn to find peace of mind, body and spirit – to chart a fresh course for the rest of my life. But as I sat in the Wembley dressing-room – correction: in the *winning team's* dressing-room at the 1987 FA Cup final (how good does it feel to say that?) – enjoying a quiet moment, I thought "This one's for me."

How close had I come to fizzling out of the game? Thankfully, we'll never know. Many players sadly do. That candle had burned so brightly when I first burst on to the scene with a succession of spectacular goals and stunning displays as part of an effervescent (though ultimately not successful) team at West Brom.

Equally, I am proud to have made an impact as one of English football's first home-grown black players – I held my chin up high and puffed out my chest in spite of the monkey chants. Unprecedented racism endured, soaked up and sent back. Thanks for the three points. See you next season! I had triumphed. The bigots and the racist bullies had not forced our burgeoning generation of black British players back into the shadows.

Battling my way into the pro game in the first place had taken an effort. Spotted playing youth football on Regent's Park – you couldn't make this stuff up. Two seasons in character-building non-League football before a fairytale move to First Division West Brom and scoring on my debut to the adulation of fans. Roy of the Rovers, move over.

It had been a journey. In some respects, I had not travelled far. I grew up mainly in north-west London, mostly on the notorious Stonebridge estate – a relative stone's throw away from Wembley. I used to ride past the stadium on the bus on my way to college while studying for my apprenticeship as an electrician.

My football life to that glorious medal-winning point had been in another urban landscape – the industrial West Midlands – in the metal-bashing Black Country with West Bromwich Albion, then Coventry, a city defined by motor car manufacturing. I would later add Aston Villa, Wolverhampton Wanderers, Wycombe Wanderers and Chester City to my roster of clubs before hanging up my boots.

Not that I was born in one of England's football-ingrained urban heartlands. The first five years of my life had been spent in French Guiana, and, briefly, the island of Saint Lucia. My parents had no grasp of England's national sport – it meant nothing to them. It wasn't part of their culture. They never took me to matches as a kid. Why would they? Not their thing. Instead they followed my career with interest from home. They hadn't even been there at Wembley that day, even though it was a short bus ride from home. Better to let someone else have the precious tickets.

Chapter One

So I had only watched maybe half a dozen live matches before making my debut with West Brom at the age of 19. Since then I'd become one of the game's first notable black players – a scorer of fantastic goals. Booed and jeered by racists, loved by the traditionalists who enjoyed seeing a powerful, free-flowing striker in full flight. I was old school – direct and instinctive. But after a bright start my career would go on the wane. I would even start drinking during the afternoons before games. Somehow I would regain my self-respect at Coventry City.

Eventually I achieved success, and all that goes with it – the cars, the women, the drinking, the swanky suburban lifestyle, the fame and adulation. But none of the rewards, or the opportunity to break the mould and become a role model, would have been possible if my dad hadn't had the guts to head for England in his late 40s with nothing but a suitcase and a desire to do right by his family.

What guts that took at that age in life! What fortitude! What character! A cup winners' medal? That's nothing by comparison. Thanks, Dad. I mean, really, truly, thanks. He did it all for us, his kids – me, my older sister and brother Nilla and Imbert, who like me were born in French Guiana, and my younger brother and sister, David and Denise, who were born in England.

Life would be an indescribable struggle – enough to test the faith and spirit of any family. At one point we were split up, living in different parts of London and beyond. Our fingers gripping tight on to the cusp of British society, our dreams of the capital's streets being paved with gold. This was the fantasy image sold in advertising by the British government to Caribbean immigrants who crammed on to boats to head to post-war Europe in search of a new life.

My mum and dad, bless them, were strong for me and my brothers and sisters. Our experience would mirror that of many Caribbean migrants. Our tale is no more noble or outstanding than most. But we would come through it with our dignity intact and with immense resolve and strength.

We were lucky – fate ultimately dealt us a good hand. Others weren't as fortunate. But equally we worked hard and were brought up the right way by our parents. We were taught the morals and ethics to do well and instilled with the desire to achieve things. We'd travelled far to succeed.

As I sat in that Wembley dressing-room, a smile of reflection spread across my face. Life can be cruel and can be tough but sometimes, like on that beautiful May afternoon in 1987, life can be sweet ... oh, so sweet.

There would be battles ahead – many of my darkest days were yet to come – but I had learned some of life's valuable lessons during the largely frustrating three-and-a-half years that preceded it. I knew I could (and would) handle what life might throw at me. I had come out on top – and football-wise at least I would never, ever have an inconsistent season again.

Ultimately I would come out of this a better man. It would be at a heavy price, but for now, with my boots, socks and shins muddied and my shirt stained with the sweat and toil of 120 minutes on Wembley's lush but strength-sapping turf, I had triumphed. Coventry City, the underdogs but a much-loved side led by our inspirational manager, John Sillett, had triumphed. And life was good.

Now, where's the bar?

CHAPTER TWO
One Gilbert Regis ...

There are two things that people often get wrong about me. One is that I am West Indian. I'm not. I am French Guianan. Oh, and my first name isn't Cyrille. Or at least it shouldn't have been. I should have been known as Gilbert. Let me explain.

I was born in the village of Maripasoula in French Guiana on 9 February 1958. My upbringing there was far removed from the bustling urban centres where I would grow up in England and play most of my football. French Guiana isn't a sunny Caribbean island with palm trees and golden sand. It is a rather large chunk of South America's north-east coast. The addition of the adjective "French" dates from colonial times, when three Guianas existed: British Guiana (now called Guyana), Dutch Guiana (now Surinam) and French Guiana, whose name has remained the same.

Not that the status of French Guiana should be confused with the other two former Guianas. Guyana and Surinam are British and Dutch colonies, but their citizens don't have the same status as those of French Guiana, which is a *département* of France, and therefore shares the same legislature and currency and head of state as any other French region. Guianans are proud to be French, as they have exactly the same rights as any Frenchman. Despite bordering Surinam to the west and Brazil to the east and south, French Guiana's currency is the Euro and European Union law applies. In fact, it is the largest land mass outside Europe to come under EU law.

Most of French Guiana's 221,000 strong population live on the northern coast, almost half of them in the suburbs surrounding the region's major city, Cayenne. Most of French Guiana's landmass is rainforest. Its main industries are fishing (which accounts for three-quarters of its foreign exports), gold mining and timber, although apparently – I've looked this up – the Guiana Space Centre at Kourou now accounts for 25 per cent of the country's Gross Domestic Product (GDP).

Historically, French Guiana is possibly best known for the infamous Devil's Island (in French *Île du Diable*), a fierce penal institution located six nautical miles off the coast, which finally closed in 1952. It was from here that former convict Henri Charrière, in his best-selling book *Papillon*, claims to have escaped, though historians have cast doubt over the validity of his story. There was a successful film of the same name in which Charrière was played by Steve McQueen.

French Guiana is split into two administrative regions or *arrondissements* and sub-divided into 22 districts or "communes". The commune of Maripasoula is geographically the largest of these communes, although the actual village of Maripasoula had no more than four or five hundred residents when I was born there in 1958. Since then the population of the village has risen to some 5,000, in line with the tenfold increase in that of French Guiana as a whole.

I am probably the most famous person to come from Maripasoula – not that I can claim to have the spirit of the place coursing through my veins. l left the village when I was a toddler and my family moved to Cayenne. I'm certainly not the best-known sportsman to hail from French Guiana. It has produced a string of top French footballers, including Bernard Lama, Florent Malouda, Marc-Antoine Fortuné and Jean-Claude Darcheville, as well as French swimmer Malia Metella. They all made their way to France – so how come I ended up in England? Indeed, quite how and why did my mum and her family and my dad end up in Maripasoula? And then how did we come to live in England rather than, say, France?

Parts of the story still remain a mystery. But here is what I know. My dad, Robert Regis, was born on 6 April 1916 as one of 15 children, including a twin sister called Eta, in a small fishing town called Canaries in St Lucia – which was a British colony, although the island also has a mixture of African, East Indian and French influence. My dad spoke Antillean Creole, a form of French patois that is still popular on the island.

Dad was a fisherman by trade, but one day his best friend was injured in a serious fishing accident and he decided to give it up. I guess, though – as with most migrations in history – economics played a major part. It was getting increasingly difficult to eke out a living in fishing, so my dad decided to try his luck prospecting for gold in the hills of French Guiana.

Doubtless there was an element of "Go west, young man" (well, go south in this case), but this was not glamorous work and huge fortunes are not made in the back-breaking endeavours to dig and pan for gold in the Amazonian rainforest, at least not by the people actually doing the digging and panning. According to research, people carrying out this gruelling work rarely earn more than the equivalent of £10 a day – though that is still incentive enough for an estimated 150,000 Brazilians to illegally hop over the border to try their luck at 1,000 clandestine mine sites today. In my dad's day it was largely unorganized. People were just given a spade and pan and a section of area to dig, and the small nuggets of gold they found would be sold to prospectors on site.

So Dad ended up living in Maripasoula. There he met my mum, Mathilde Gladys Fadaire, who was 17 years old when she met him, and 17 years younger than Dad, who was then 34. By all accounts he was also a bit of a charmer. He loved dancing – especially the merengue, a Latin American dance in which partners hold each other closely – and he liked his nightclubs – not that the nightlife in Maripasoula was particularly exotic, extensive or exciting. As it was a rural backwater with a tiny population, most of the folks there were older. My mum was one of the few young women around, so it was a quite natural attraction. In their respective ways, they were quite a catch for each other.

My dad already had three children in St Lucia: Joseph (who we know as "Cools") who now lives in Canada; Theresa-Mary, who still lives in St Lucia; and Marcellina, who ironically now lives in Paddington, West London – not far from where we lived after moving to England in 1963. It's a small world, and although we didn't grow up together we have always stayed in touch.

Dad was also extremely muscly. In fact, my mum used to call him Big Russia, because of his huge muscular frame. This was a natural characteristic I inherited from my old man. When I first burst on to the English football scene in 1977, many people assumed I had built my muscle mass either from working on building sites (I was an apprentice electrician) or working out in gyms – which back in the 1970s before the days of modern gyms and health clubs was almost unheard of. I was even accused of wearing shirts that were too small to accentuate my physique. As if.

At West Brom we only had a small weights room, and all it held was a collection of rusty old iron dumb-bells that had been around since Noah's time. No, much to the irritation and annoyance of fellow sportsmen and fitness freaks who work hard pumping iron to achieve a ripped torso, for me it was all totally natural – inherited from my father, Robert, whose own physique was doubtless honed in the hills and gold mines of French Guiana.

There is a downside, of course. Although I had a strong physique, natural pace and speed, I lacked stamina. If you are heavily muscled you slow down quickly and, physiologically, you are easily sapped of energy. Ron Atkinson, my manager at West Brom and Aston Villa, used to jokingly call me "59 Yards", because I was the world's worst long-distance runner. I had power and pace but no endurance – which meant that in time I had to learn to manage my game accordingly.

My mum's family came from the island of Guadeloupe in the eastern Caribbean, another French *département* which, like French Guiana, bizarrely comes under European Union law and has the Euro as its currency.

My grandmother was one of 13 children, and was given away by her mum and dad to an uncle whose wife couldn't have kids. Today this may sound an incredibly harsh thing to do, but it was more common in those days. It has been the cause of much upset for my grandmother – who, at the time of writing this book, is still alive. She hasn't been back to Guadeloupe, because it is too painful for her, but she is planning to return for her sister's 100th birthday in July 2010.

Quite why they ended up moving to French Guiana is a mystery and a missing part of my family's story. Maybe my old friend and Baggies fan Adrian Chiles, who used to present BBC1's *Who Do You Think You Are?* could get their researchers to look at it – because I would love to know!

Anyway, they settled in Maripasoula, where my grandma got pregnant at 18 and had a falling out with her family. So when my mum was born on 30 January 1934 she left her with the same uncle that had brought grandma to French Guiana. Although I know a bit about my mum's family, it is sad that I don't know much about my cousins or my family's background, but you cannot let the past rule your present or future.

Not long after moving in together, Mum and Dad had the first of five children when my eldest sister, Nilla, was born in 20 March 1952. Nilla is almost six years older than me and four years older than my brother Imbert, who was born on 12 May 1956. By the time I came along on 9 February 1958, my dad was 42 years old and my mum was 24.

But I wasn't supposed to be *Cyrille* Regis. In French culture you have a first name that comes from the saint you were born under; then the name your parents give you; then, thirdly, your family name. So just as Nilla's first name is Guillaumette, and Imbert's is Nera, then my name should have been Cyrille (after St Cyrille) Gilbert Regis. So I'd be known as Gilbert [pronounced jeel-bare].

At least that was the plan. The trouble was that Maripasoula, being such a small village, didn't have a place where births, deaths and marriages could be registered. You had to travel along one of the many long estuaries by boat to Cayenne, the capital, to do that. Back then in the 1950s, there were no railways and few roads. However, a family friend was travelling to Cayenne, so my parents asked him to register my birth. Apparently, by the time he got to the capital he could remember my first name but had forgotten my second name, so he ended up giving the clerk just the one forename on my birth certificate, which reads "Cyrille Regis".

For the first five years of my life, indeed until the time we moved to England in 1963, I was actually known as Gilbert. But when we arrived in the UK with my birth certificate bearing the name "Cyrille", my mum insisted I was to be called that, so there wouldn't be any confusion or problems with the authorities. However, when I go back to French Guiana my grandmother still calls me Gilbert. Bless her, she is now in her 90s and doesn't know me by any other name. So I could have been Gilbert, Gil, Gilly or maybe even Bert – who knows? One Gilbert Regis … it has a certain ring, don't you think?

One thing is for sure – the originality of being called Cyrille in England, as distinct from the more common English version, Cyril, has ultimately served me well down the years. No one ever says, "Oh, you know whatsisname Regis"… they usually remember my full name. I don't recall being ribbed much about it when I was a kid, either. I guess some of this may have been because I was good at sport – especially football, cricket and running. Children don't tend to tease you when you can play sport well … and you're bigger than they are!

The urban life I would eventually lead in West London and cities in the West Midlands would be a stark contrast to

Maripasoula. I have few recollections of living there – just vague memories of a rough track for a road and running around naked in the humid sub-equatorial Amazon rainforest heat. In those conditions what's the point of wearing clothes that will become sticky and constantly get wet?

Apparently Maripasoula didn't even have a school, so we moved away when I was small. My sister Nilla had already left when she was four or five to live with an uncle in Cayenne, so that she could attend school. Cayenne was a day's journey by boat away, so she didn't see the rest of us for a couple of years, until she was about seven or eight, when the family moved there. French Guiana is also, quite obviously, French-speaking – and Nilla grew up speaking "proper" French. At home we spoke patois – which is broken French mixed with bits of other linguistic influences from Africa and Europe. In Cayenne we lived in a wooden shack, and I recall jumping into the hammock where our dad slept when he wasn't around. We would also pick mangoes, bananas and other fruits from the trees and just eat them outside. The ditch through the road we lived on served as an open sewer. A few years ago when I went back I walked down the road where we lived. It had changed for the better and now had proper sanitation.

I also remember a funeral in Cayenne when I was three or four years old. It was for a man called Catayée, the country's prefect who died in a plane crash. He was a much loved and respected man, and to French Guianans it was as traumatic as President John F. Kennedy's assassination. We followed the procession along its route.

Being away from our parents affected Nilla. She was a tomboy, and by her own admission was a rebellious and naughty child. She hated being away from her family – but she had more of it to come, as soon we would head for my dad's homeland of St Lucia without her.

Times were tough. The arduous search for gold wasn't bringing in enough money to feed a growing family of five – so at the age of 46 my dad took the enormously brave decision to head to Europe, and England in particular, to seek out a fresh life. It was the best way, as he and Mum saw it, of giving their family a better future. Dad had a British passport which meant he could emigrate to England, where there was plenty of work. After marrying Mum in 1961, he would be able to get the rest of us to join him in the UK. First he had to find work, so that he could afford the fare for all of us.

This was a brave venture. He was a labourer, so he didn't have a trade, and he was in his mid-40s. Who can guess at the thoughts and emotions swirling through my dad's head and the stirrings in his heart as he boarded the boat to England to seek out a new life in a strange, far-off continent? My dad, like so many folks of his generation, wasn't touchy-feely and never felt the need to spill his guts or reveal how he was thinking or feeling about life. But it was an unbelievably brave, gutsy, unselfish thing to do at an age when most are looking to settle and put down some roots.

When I became a professional footballer and was living in a smart four-bedroom house in Sutton Coldfield, a leafy West Midlands town close to Birmingham, with two cars on the drive, was able to take regular foreign holidays and buy opulent presents for the kids and was a household name and an international footballer, I wrote to Dad to simply say "thanks". I had just become a Christian and was reflecting on my life. I wrote to thank him for being there for us –

for not running out on his responsibilities, for giving us the chance to have a better life in a strange continent. Many men couldn't cope. We went through tremendous problems but my dad never shirked his responsibilities. I was grateful for that and wanted him to know. I didn't want it unsaid any longer. There's too much of that in life.

He came to the UK with nothing but managed to create a future for all of us. Thankfully – although, as you will read, it wasn't without an immense struggle and heart-rending difficulties – each of us was able to seize most of the opportunity afforded us by our wonderful loving, caring parents, who endured almost unbelievable and unspeakable heartache in the process.

My dad never said a lot. Many men were like that back then – but he just wanted the best for his children. All I can say here and now to both Mum and Dad, who died within six weeks of each other in 1999 and 2000, is "Thank you. Thank you so much from the bottom of my heart – and from my brothers' and sisters' hearts too." Even though they are no longer with us, their sacrifice of seeking out a new life in England is never far from my thoughts.

Although there were fears at the time about the UK being "swamped" by migrants – often stirred up by British right-wing politicians (and notoriously, of course, by Enoch Powell in his "Rivers of Blood" speech in which he predicted "the black man holding the whip hand over the white man"), it should be noted that migrants from countries like French Guiana and Surinam also headed for France and the Netherlands, so this was not just a British thing.

People from the Caribbean weren't desperate to get to the UK in order to get their hands on social security payments, as was often claimed, and little else. As with any mass migrations throughout history it was fuelled by a desire to find work and forge a new life – and that is what the vast majority of people did. Work was drying up in the Caribbean, and Europe was rebuilding after the devastation of the Second World War. Work was there.

Immigration from the West Indies was encouraged by the British Nationality Act of 1948, which gave all Commonwealth citizens free entry into Britain. The symbolic starting point of this mass migration to the "mother country" was the journey of the *SS Empire Windrush* from Jamaica in June 1948. Half a million people left the Caribbean to live and work in Britain between 1948 and 1970. They were British citizens and had actually been invited to come, by businesses such as London Transport. Dad moved to England and settled in West London close to where his three brothers Fergus, Harrison and Lennox had also arrived. Meanwhile Mum, Imbert and I moved to St Lucia, staying with Dad's twin sister Eta in Canaries, the small fishing town where he had grown up. Once again Nilla, by now 10 years old, was split from the family, staying in French Guiana until she got the call to join us in 1964. Me, Mum and Imbert joined my dad in the UK early in 1963, a year after he went, but first there was the serious business of fun.

My memories of the year I spent in St Lucia are of absolute freedom. I went to school for one year – but mainly it was the enjoyment of playing on the beach and on jetties with my brother Imbert and Eta's son Papuo that I remember. It was fantastic – though looking back with the benefit of hindsight it must also have been a nerve-wracking struggle for my mum. She didn't know what was happening to her husband and she had three children to support.

By trade she was a seamstress – though I don't recall her working. Mum could make dresses and any other type of clothing but it was hard on her too. In St Lucia she didn't know anyone outside my dad's family and must have had concerns about her husband, who was 17 years older and living and working in another continent.

Meanwhile, my dad was trying to find whatever work he could in London. He was unskilled, so found jobs as a labourer. He had worked hard all his life, and that continued in England, where sometimes he had two jobs at the same time to put food on the table. Manual labour was low paid, so it was always a struggle for Dad – which is why, years later, he was always so keen for us to get trades, so we could make our own way in life. He had been a labourer all his life – doing hard physical work, in gold mines, in factories, as a fisherman – so he wanted better for us. A trade would do that and offer economic opportunities.

He came to England sold on the dream of the streets paved with gold. Most people thought that if they worked hard and built up some money, then 15 to 20 years later they would be able to return home to retire. Few managed that. Migrants throughout history have been driven by a desire for a better life – because one line of work is ending and others seem to be about to start. But Dad managed to get a foothold in Britain – even if it was a very slender one, as we were soon to find out. In West London to be precise, Swinging London as it was soon to be, the epicentre of the pop culture that would make the 1960s an exciting time – though not necessarily for us.

Eventually we got the call to join Dad. Somehow he had scraped together the money to bring us over. Our new life was about to begin.

CHAPTER THREE
Swinging London

Just as tropical rainstorms are an abiding memory of my formative years in French Guiana, so my early memories of living in London are dominated by rain. A different type of rain, though. Not warm tropical storms to cool you down. Cold rain. Damp, dank drizzle. Not the sort you could dance around naked in.

One of my earliest memories of life in England is staring out of the window into the back garden of the first flat where we lived in London, with water gushing from a broken pipe at the back of the building and rain hammering down on to the grimy, grey exterior. I couldn't believe we had left the sunny Caribbean for this.

Mum, Imbert and I set sail for England in February 1963. I was five years old. It was a two-week boat journey – which may seem incredible in the modern age of cheap plane travel when most destinations in the world are reachable within hours.

I have a vivid memory of looking back at St Lucia – at the palm trees and the beach. Of seeing little bits of flotsam dancing in the sea around the ripples of the boat we were travelling on. It would be my last sight of the Caribbean – its pale green sea, golden sands, green trees and blue skies – for 20 years.

The boat we came to England on was called *Ascania*

Two. It was a Cunard line ship packed with people like us –
families heading for a thrilling new life in England. The three
of us shared a cabin. Imbert and I whiled away the journey
having great fun playing on the deck, running around, barely
noticing the hours and days slipping by. It was exciting. We
had no sense of anticipation, no fear or trepidation over what
might greet us or what life might be like in England.

I was five. England, like Europe, was just a name to me
really. I had no conception of what it might be like. Everywhere
in the world was surely like Guiana or St Lucia? I didn't know
it was going to be cold. To be honest, I didn't know what
cold was – but I was about to find out. I hadn't even spoken
English until I came over to England either. All of this was
going to be new to me. To Imbert and me, this was simply a
great big adventure.

Neither did I have any idea about what a monumental
event this was for our mum. How must she have felt about
leaving without her daughter? Nilla was older than us and
eventually came over when she was 12 years old.

I can vaguely remember the boat docking at the massive port
of Southampton and then taking the train to Waterloo, one of
London's busiest railway stations. Can you imagine what it looked
and sounded like to a little kid from Maripasoula? French Guiana
and St Lucia had very little transport infrastructure. Glancing
upwards at the grandeur of its huge iron and glass roof had me
spellbound. I was goggle-eyed. The noise seemed incredible. It
was deafening. I remember thinking, "I'll never get used to this."
Everything seems bigger when you are a kid, doesn't it?

I don't remember the journey to our first home. Apparently
it was by bus. But the address is burned into my memory

– 383 Portobello Road. It was a Victorian three-storey town house, converted into one-bedroom maisonettes. The houses on that stretch of Portobello Road had one room at the front on the right-hand side as you entered the building. Four of us lived in a single room, where Dad had been living on his own. It was a dump. Horrible. This did not seem like the England we'd heard about – with all its finery and riches.

London was grey, cold and colourless but incredibly busy. We'd come from sunshine and lush greenery – with beaches, palm trees, space to play. Portobello Road, with its well-established market, seemed to sum up London – all hustle and bustle.

I've checked. In February 1963 Frank Ifield was number one in the pop charts with "The Wayward Wind", soon to be replaced by Cliff Richard's "Summer Holiday". The Profumo Affair (kids, ask your mums and dads) was rocking the British establishment and the nation's sensibilities. But the Swinging Sixties with London at the epicentre of a cultural phenomenon were yet to kick into gear.

Although we lived in West London, in the Royal Borough of Kensington and Chelsea – in fact in what is now the very well-to-do and sought-after area of Notting Hill – little, if any, of that glitz and glamour rubbed off on the dwellings of Portobello Road, even if it was the fictional setting for the Walt Disney musical, *Bedknobs and Broomsticks*.

Ours was a less cosy image of West London. We moved slap-bang into the area from where the notorious post-war landlord Peter Rachman ran his empire, although our maisonette was not one of his properties. His tactic of maximizing the rent from his properties by packing them full of African-Caribbean immigrants, often driving out the mostly white sitting tenants in Notting Hill who had statutory protection against high rent increases, has become folklore. New tenants such as ourselves did not have the same protection under the law, so could be charged any amount Rachman wished. Most of the new tenants were immigrants who had no choice but to accept the high rents because it was difficult to obtain housing elsewhere in London.

Whether actually violent or not, unscrupulous landlords often used the threat of violence to drive out sitting tenants, and houses were subdivided into a number of small flats in order to increase the number of tenancies without rent controls. The older residents, meanwhile, felt threatened by the change in the area. This was an era when it was commonplace to see signs saying: "No blacks, No dogs, No Irish" in the windows of properties to let.

We spent the first five months of our life in England living in a one-room flat. I can still remember Imbert and me playing in the cupboard and, kids being kids – with an endless appetite to make the most of any potential play situation – my brother locking me in there. No wonder I am still slightly claustrophobic nowadays. I think it stems from that time.

It was just our luck too to move to England in the Big Freeze. This was Britain's coldest snap for decades, lasting from Christmas to early March, with record low temperatures at night, regular snowfalls and thick ice. Lovely when you've come from a climate where even at night time temperatures rarely drop below 20 degrees Celsius.

I had to get used to cold, rain, snow, ice, traffic, busy streets – and school, which also meant mastering English as quickly as possible, having been brought up as a French speaker.

Although we would converse in patois at home, we would always speak English away from the house. This was partly because we considered it rude to others for us to be speaking in patois, but also to encourage us to communicate and assimilate as quickly as possible. Gradually we all began to talk in English all of the time. It was a tactic that worked wonderfully, as it speeded up our grasp of English and allowed us to settle in at school more quickly.

In July 1963 we moved to 6 Peploe Road, Kensal Rise, not far from Portobello Road. Thankfully, it was slightly leafier and more upmarket. We had a flat on the second floor with two rooms – one of them at the front with a bay window – and a cooker on the landing, which we shared with another family. We also had a communal toilet. The owner lived downstairs directly beneath us.

Although, in theory, we should have had more space, our family expanded from four to seven in the space of two years. Firstly Nilla came over to join us in March 1964 via a brief spell of living in St Lucia. Around the same time, my younger brother David was born, and a year later, in May 1965, my sister Denise arrived. This all made for some very compact sleeping arrangements. I slept in a double bed in the front room with Imbert, and Nilla slept in a camp-bed. David slept with Mum and Dad, with Denise in a cot.

Despite being raised as a French speaker, Nilla took to London life really well, and eventually became a prefect and head girl at Chamberlayne Road School in Kensal Rise – we were really proud of her.

There was a great communal feel around Kensal Rise. At the nearby sweet shop you could buy things on tick if you didn't have the money. And there was a lovely old-fashioned grocer's shop 50 yards down the road, which meant we could run errands from a young age.

Being short of space, we made the most of the facilities around us. During school holidays Mum would shout, "Get out of the house!" – which left us with two main options, playing in the street or trotting down to nearby Queen's Park, which was just 400 yards away.

The streets around Peploe Road were built in a block – and one of our friends had a bike. I didn't have a bike until I was 14 and then I had to make it myself. So we used to borrow his and race around the block to see who could cover it the fastest.

Queen's Park was lots of fun for us youngsters. It had a canteen, a park warden who kept an eye on everyone, conker trees – and it was ours. The park was the centre of our community. We spent hours, even whole days, there sometimes – climbing trees, running around playing games – all kinds of things that kept us fit, active and healthy without our even realizing we were exercising. It didn't matter what time the park opened or closed because we could squeeze in through the iron gates.

I'm sure we probably did some mischievous things too, but it is the happy, imaginative games and the good times that I remember most. We went out day after day to have fun, and because there were lots of other kids doing the same it was all the more enjoyable. With my mates I'd go around the park collecting Coke and Pepsi bottles, bringing them back for a tanner – a couple of pence in today's money – to make a little bit of cash which we probably spent on sweets. We knew the park warden and he knew us, so we never had to worry about any trouble. There weren't any gangs, or people taking drugs or drinking alcohol and alienating others.

It was safe, fun and a fundamental part of our upbringing. Quite what we would have done without it heaven only knows. Sadly, many of our parks are the reverse these days. Some inner-city parks have become almost the sole preserve of gangs who intimidate people in a bunch of different ways. People are often frightened to use parks even though they're a vital communal resource.

Initially I went to a school in Ladbroke Grove, but when we moved to Peploe Road I went to Kensal Rise Primary School, between the ages of six and 11 (albeit with one brief gap which I will come on to later). It was only a short bus ride away. Ours was a multi-racial area – and our school reflected that. There were lots of kids from different backgrounds who got along perfectly fine.

The school didn't mix up the genders, though. Kensal Rise Primary is on three levels – infants taught on the ground floor, girls on the first floor and boys on the second floor. Indeed I sat through single-sex lessons throughout my entire schooling as I went on to a Roman Catholic secondary school.

At home, things were difficult. There was lots of love in our house, and Mum and Dad always tried to bring us up in the best way possible – but we were always short of money. Not because my dad didn't work hard. He worked as a labourer at Wall's Sausages in Park Royal, and for about six months he also had a second part-time job in the evening, but he had to give that up because it was too tiring for him.

He was trying to get enough money together so we could buy a house. Sadly, he never achieved it. Consequently I have few early childhood memories of my dad. He was rarely around. Not because he was out living it up, drinking and smoking away the money he'd earned – but because he would often get home after we'd gone to bed.

As in most households, Mum was the economist. Dad took out his bus fare and lunch money from his pay packet, then gave the rest to my mum, who set the household budgets, paid the bills, bought the groceries and clothes and gave us our pocket money. Naturally she couldn't go out to work as she was looking after Denise and David, who hadn't yet reached school age, but she would do sewing at home, taking in piece work. An Asian man used to come round with a bagful of collars, sleeves and cuffs for Mum to put together.

For a time we didn't have a television. One of my first television memories, when we did, was watching Winston Churchill's funeral in 1965 and witnessing the grief of the entire nation. I don't remember the World Cup in 1966 even though it was in England. All of England's matches and the final were played at Wembley Stadium, just a few miles away. At the time I was more interested in cricket, because that was the sport I was best at and played most at school.

But things were about to get whole lot worse for the Regis family. As the so-called summer of love drew to a close in 1967 we had a row with our landlord. Living directly beneath us, he got fed up with the noise we made and kept complaining. It wasn't that we shouted a lot or played loud music, but there were five of us kids and it was inevitable that we made noise by jumping about and generally being boisterous. He had a daughter, so maybe it was affecting her sleep. He used to get a broom handle and bang it on his ceiling in frustration. Eventually he asked us to leave.

With nowhere to go we applied for housing through Brent Council, but they didn't have anywhere for a family of seven. At the time, with the huge programme of building new housing estates and council blocks yet to get into full swing, Britain's housing stock was poor.

For a short time we moved into a hostel at 91 Dartmouth Road in Willesden. Men weren't allowed to stay there, so my dad went to live with his brother, Fergus. So it was Mum and us five kids. At first we were in a big dormitory with lots of other families; then, after a couple of weeks, we got two rooms to ourselves.

I get upset when I think about what my mum and dad went through and how stressed and frustrated they must have been. As the clock ticked down, I can just imagine them saying to each other: "Is this what we came here for?" They came to Britain to elevate themselves but found themselves and their children living in a dormitory. Can you imagine their feelings of failure, even though they had done nothing wrong except be poor in a society that values wealth above most other things?

Later on, Mum told me she always held it together for us kids. We didn't know of her hurt, though we could imagine. It went unspoken. But she often used to cry when she was on her own.

As for Dad – well, how did he feel when he was unable to be with his family? Respect to him though, he stayed. Other dads didn't and still don't. I thank him for that. You think of the things you go through as a man and the things your parents sacrificed for you to give you a chance – and the pain that must have been going on their minds and in their hearts.

When we left the Caribbean they thought this would be a brave new adventure in the capital city at the heart of the Commonwealth, and everything in their lives would be up and away. Now we were reduced to living apart from our dad and in a dormitory, with no privacy from other families.

Throughout these troubled times, I still travelled to school on the bus – and I really enjoyed it. Sport was a blessed relief from our housing problems. I played cricket and football for the school and I was good at another competition – throwing the cricket ball. I could hurl it the entire length of the playground.

But our lives were to take another turn for the worse. Once we had to leave the hostel the only option was for us to be split up until suitable accommodation became available. Dad carried on living with Uncle Fergus. Poor Nilla was once again separated from the family and went to live in a children's home in Cricklewood, so she could continue her schooling at Chamberlayne. Mum, Imbert and Denise went to live in a Salvation Army hostel in Mile End, over on the other side of London, and David and I were sent to stay, believe it or not, in a convent in Aldershot, way out in Hampshire.

We were apart for nine months. At times it would seem like a lot longer.

Convents and Council Houses

My brother David used to talk in his sleep and would chatter away about all kinds of things, doubtlessly dreaming of happier times. Being separated from the rest of the family was traumatic, and this was his way of coping. He was only two when we were split up and was so desperately upset.

He would cry his eyes out for hours after Mum came to the convent to visit us – and the sobs of my inconsolable little brother wanting our mother and our family to be reunited again used to ring in my ears. At the end of her visits Mum couldn't let him see she was leaving, because he would get so upset. She'd have to leave when he was distracted. David and I have a special bond because of the time we spent together. I had to be his stronger older brother and had to learn to take responsibility for him, because he was my brother and was so young. He used to follow me everywhere.

I also had to learn to control my feelings. I couldn't let him see that I too was upset. If I lost my temper he would too. "It'll be alright, David," I would say to him constantly. "It will be alright."

When I played professional football later, people used to notice that I didn't seem to react to abuse or respond to a bit of verbal from a defender who was trying to rile me. It's true that I wasn't easily wound up, and I wonder if it stems from that time. As a footballer, I could channel my anger into my performance.

For nine months David and I lived at St Anthony's Convent, which was run by the Franciscan Missionaries of the Divine Motherhood, in Aldershot, Hampshire, and we were educated there too. I also took part in local sports competitions.

Although we were very upset at not being with our family – and of course we constantly wondered what life was like for them – I have to admit we had a fantastic time. The nuns were great with us. They were all lovely people, full of the milk of human kindness. There were loads of kids like David and me there, maybe 30 or so, and they were brilliant at looking after all of us. It was a true home for kids in our position.

By that time, I was already aware of faith and religion. I was raised as a Roman Catholic – many Caribbean folks are. I had my first Holy Communion at the age of seven. But God was just an abstract figure. I didn't feel I had a personal relationship with Him.

My mum used to pray all the time and would speak to God as she wandered around the house, so I was kind of used to a sense of a God being all around us. Most Caribbean family homes will have a picture of Jesus Christ somewhere and we were no different. But at that stage of my life it meant little more than that.

At Easter, I remember the nuns brought in this huge chocolate egg for all the girls and boys. They took a great big wooden spoon and cracked the egg open. Our eyes grew wider as we saw it was full of chocolate, and then we all ate some. They looked after us well and we had a really good time there.

Chapter Four

Because I was so good at sport, I was allowed to travel to nearby Farnborough to compete in inter-school races, and I tore it up – beating everybody in sight. I won certificates and school titles in both the 100 and 200 metres.

I also enjoyed playing on the wide open common, which gave me a sense of freedom. I remember the heady smell of rhododendron bushes and the little dragonflies hovering around. This helped relieve some of the aching sadness I was feeling. As long as I was occupied it was a happy time for me.

But the same couldn't be said for my mum. She was staying at a Salvation Army hostel in the East End of London with Imbert and Denise. They had to be in by 6pm each evening and out by 6am in the morning.

That was my mum's lowest time. She would take Imbert to school but then had to look after Denise all day. She usually spent her days on a park bench, crying and wondering if things would work out for all of us. Occasionally she would spend some time at the house of a friend from St Lucia called Theresa, but for the most part she'd be sitting on her own in floods of tears. In later life she told me that it was during this period that her faith leapt to another level.

She would pray that the family would be reunited and that everything would be alright. As a little girl growing up in the village of Maripasoula in French Guiana she had to walk through the woods on her own at the tender age of five. So she would pray that she would be safe. She developed a relationship with God as a child and felt comfortable talking to Him.

One day, as she sat on that park bench, she had this feeling that everything would be OK. Something happened. God told her that things would be alright. She never cried after that. Years later I would have a similar experience that would change my life too.

My sister Nilla, who was still living in a children's home in Cricklewood, so she could continue her schooling at Chamberlayne, was fairly close to Dad as he was staying with his brother Fergus in Ladbroke Grove in West London. But Nilla only met up with Mum once or twice during the whole nine months we were apart. David and I didn't see any of our family other than Mum for that entire time, because we simply couldn't afford the bus or train fares.

Mum's faith was eventually repaid. Our family was reunited and this time we had our own house, albeit in a road that was earmarked for demolition. Not that the Regis family were remotely concerned about this potentially alarming development. We were together as a family again and although, in some respects, I was sad to leave the freedom of the convent, it was for all the right reasons. We were beginning a new chapter in our lives – we were back together as a family and things would start to turn for us, at last.

Brent Council found us a place to live in Stonebridge – at 116 Barry Road. We knew it was temporary, because the council was already moving people out of Barry Road to make way for the huge new Stonebridge housing estate which was being built nearby. No. 116 was an old house – two up, two down, with an outdoor toilet and no bath – but it was our home. It was in an avenue and there was plenty of greenery around.

There was a derelict shop one side and an elderly couple living on the other side. We could use the derelict garden and, boy, we made the most of that after all we'd been through. We didn't have a bathroom, so we either had to use a tin bath or have a stand-up wash, a "wipe down" as we called it. Once a week we used to catch the bus to Paddington to go to the public baths at Halfpenny Steps.

At Barry Road, my mum and dad slept in one room. Denise was with them. Nilla had a small room at the back of the house, Imbert and I shared a bed, and David was in a single bed. We stayed at Barry Road for two or three years, then moved on to the newly opened Stonebridge estate.

Stonebridge developed an unenviable reputation, but when it first opened it was a great place for people like ourselves, who had struggled to find affordable housing. This was at the peak of the post-war housing boom, when there was genuine demand to increase and modernize the country's housing stock. Sometimes people get dewy-eyed about the past and blame many of the things that have gone in society on the construction of huge blocks of council flats. But as far as we were concerned, as kids, it was great to live there at that time.

We lived at 23 Palmers Court. We had more space than we'd had before. I remember being blown away – it seemed so massive and luxurious. Our flat had four bedrooms, two inside toilets and a bath. I finally had my own bed. At last we had hot running water, a bathroom and indoor toilets.

It was comfortable housing for families similar to ourselves who had struggled to gain a proper foothold in London, and a community feeling soon developed. It meant something and it was new. There was also a park to play in. Just like before, we would go out and play all day and hang around until 11pm at night. Most families regularly chatted to each other and everyone got on.

Recently, I attended the funeral of Junior Roberts, my nephew

Jason Roberts's uncle on his father's side and the brother of Fitzroy Roberts, who is mentioned later in this book. There I met a family who had been in the dormitory with us at that time and had also moved on to Stonebridge. Everyone from the old days was there. It was great to see people from a long way back. Jason's father's family lived in Stonebridge too.

In later years, Stonebridge developed a reputation as a no-go area, synonymous with the worst of high-rise council estates. Some of the blocks have been knocked down and huge efforts have been made to turn things around in recent years – but there is no doubt the estate is rough and tough. But it wasn't always that way. It gave us stability and a roof over our heads. I will never forget that.

Everyone seemed to be buying stereograms and turntables. Dad was a big Jim Reeves man. The front room of our Caribbean house was a colourful sight. Nothing matched – this was the 1970s! – and we had ornate glasses that we hardly ever drank from and, after years of absolutely no space, we now we had a room that was kept for best and rarely used. Typical. We were a family at last with a place in English society. We'd arrived.

By this time I had moved on to secondary school. Cardinal Hinsley School in Harlesden was an all-boys Catholic school. I used to catch the No. 18 bus from Harrow Road to Harlesden Coliseum and walk up the hill to school.

Going to a Catholic school and church gave me a deeper awareness of God and Jesus, which was important later on in my life. I went to Mass until I was about 13 and also went to confession, but then I gradually stopped. Like all young guys I wanted to be out with my mates, but Mum always insisted that we went to church. Although, as I've said, Caribbean houses usually have a picture of Jesus Christ, I didn't have faith in God at that point. It was too much of an abstract concept. I was too young to fully understand who God was. At that age you go to church to please your parents, in my case my mum, rather than through conviction.

I went back to Cardinal Hinsley recently to hand out certificates at a presentation night. It has changed – it's now a technology college – but it still felt awesome to go back to my old school. I enjoyed my time there and had a nice group of friends.

People often ask me if racism played a part in my upbringing. I am not going to pretend we were immune to it, but I don't remember too many incidents. I recall seeing signs saying "No blacks, No dogs, No Irish", and the pained reaction on my parents' faces, but I learned to live with it. Talking to Nilla, I realize that my parents protected us from a lot of their negative experiences.

When I moved into my teens I became wary of gangs and aware of seeing black kids sticking with black kids and white kids with white kids. Racism, like many things, is learned behaviour. The kids who had racist views picked them up from others, but that doesn't happen at primary school because they wouldn't have known what it meant.

On the sporting side, I was better at cricket than football when I was at primary school. Although I was in the school football team at 10 and 11, I didn't stand out as being super talented. At Kensal Rise Primary, we had an Australian teacher who taught us to play cricket. I played for the Borough of Brent at cricket at Under-11 level and was mainly a bowler.

I was one of the bigger lads but I wasn't the tallest boy around. I didn't throw my weight around. In fact, I can only remember having one fight at school through my entire schooldays, which is probably less than most kids.

As well as cricket, I remember competing for both my schools in inter-school athletics competitions. My specialities were the 100 metres and later the javelin.

At Cardinal Hinsley, we played football in the packed playground – 20 or more a side with a busted football, basically a flat ball. I didn't get into the school team until I was 12 or 13. I wasn't a natural pick for the sports master.

There was no history of football in our family. I don't remember watching the 1966 World Cup, in spite of all the excitement in England, but four years later the Mexico World Cup was a wake-up call. Watching the Brazilians' silky skills was a wonderful experience and really fired my imagination.

I never had a deep-down desire to become a footballer. I just loved playing the game with my mates. I liked the camaraderie of sport, the banter and the social side. Quite Corinthian, I guess! I recall leaving school early to play against other schools in Willesden, Kilburn and Harlesden – it was fun to travel on the bus together and to feel part of a team.

Somehow I ended up playing up front. If a ball was played over the top I would chase it. Because I was fast, no one could catch me. I was 13 and 14 when this happened and I gradually found my best position – as a striker. Fortunately, I was also blessed with a natural ability to score goals. We could be playing badly but I could still turn nothing into something. I had power and pace. I certainly stood out even though I didn't have any technical graces.

We had a good school team, and I was up front banging in goals. We won some trophies, but I never thought of becoming a professional footballer. It wasn't on the horizon and didn't seem mapped out for me. And I never wrote to clubs for trials, unlike some of the other lads and their parents. To me, it was just fun.

We played a lot of our matches at King Edward's Park, which was a 10-minute walk away. I recall playing against Luther Blissett there. I knew his name because he was a very good player and well known in the borough. Luther became an apprentice at Watford, and when I started work a few years later I used to see him on the train wearing his tracksuit, heading for Vicarage Road, while I was carrying my toolbox, wearing a donkey jacket and Dr Martens boots, heading for a building site in London somewhere.

One of our school sports masters at Cardinal Hinsley was Terry Marsden, who also ran the Brent borough team. I represented the borough but not the county side. Another sports teacher, Ken Ward, taught me between the ages of 13 and 15. When I bumped into Ken recently, he recalled that I was an imposing player with a natural athletic physique and that I excelled at many sports, not just football but athletics, especially sprinting and the javelin.

"You could have eaten anyone alive," Ken told me – but the thing that impressed him most was my temperament. Despite my size, I wasn't intimidating. I was laid back, easy-going and popular with my peers. "Nothing would anger you. It's one of the reasons why you did so well as a professional footballer, because you wouldn't let defenders get on top of you," said Ken.

Ken was surprised, all those years ago, to hear I'd been signed by West Brom, and at how quickly it seemed to happen, because at school I didn't seem that ambitious. It is very different today when there is so much competition to find the best young players, and clubs attract children into their teams from an early age. Ken says he enjoyed teaching me and that he felt that having me in his class was a gift because I was so enthusiastic and popular.

Over the years I have been back to the school on a couple of occasions for presentation nights, and I always take time to speak to all the young people. Being a role model to them is important.

I didn't just play schools football. I played for a team called Carmel Hall at the Catholic church I attended – the Five Precious Wounds – which had a social club in the basement. People would go straight from church to the social club to have a few beers. There was a youth club based there too.

Outside school, football began to take up more and more of my leisure time. We would play five-a-side football and table tennis in youth clubs all over north-west London.

For a while I joined Ryder Brent Valley, which would prove an inspirational club later on, but at 14 and 15 I also played for Oxford and Kilburn, which was a youth club, sometimes known as the OK Club, run by a chap called Dave Watson. I played there alongside future England cricket captain Mike Gatting and his brother Steve, who played for Arsenal, Brighton and Charlton. Mike was a bit older, but we played in the same team for two years. Both brothers were great table tennis players too.

Another future top footballer around at that time was

Ricky Hill, who attended John Kelly High School. Ricky, a midfielder, was a year younger than me, but everybody in the borough was talking about him as a future professional, as they would with all the kids who stood out. The first time we met was when Ricky's Sunday League team, The Hub, played against Ryder Brent Valley.

Ryder Brent Valley were lucky to receive some sponsorship money and, as a result, were one of the most prestigious youth teams in the area. Our players were always immaculately turned out. Ricky told me he recalls me being this huge centre-forward built like a man-mountain, a man among boys who could sprint and shoot. Ricky said he was certain that I'd make it as a professional footballer, which is funny because that is precisely what I was thinking about him. Ricky stood out too. We were truly blessed to have so many good players playing in Brent around that time, including myself, Ricky, Luther Blissett, Steve Gatting and Dave Beasant, the future Wimbledon goalkeeper – who all went on to become top-class professionals.

I bumped into Ricky years later when he was at Luton Town and he reminded me of it recently. When he was still a teenager, I told him he had so much skill that he was bound to make the grade. That really inspired him because, although he had been at Luton for two years by the time I signed for West Brom, I played top-flight football before he did as Luton were in the Second Division at that time. But it seems my words of encouragement helped give Ricky the belief that he could go on to bigger and better things – which of course he did. He became a Luton legend and played three times for England.

In fact, we later found ourselves together in the England set-up. I took Ricky under my wing and made sure he was comfortable with everything. As far as I'm concerned, we're still the same boys who played youth football together.

Not that keeping up with the kids who had the smartest kit and best boots was easy. My mum and dad weren't like some of the other parents who would buy the latest snazzy boots for their boys on a regular basis and drove them to matches in the family car. That sort of support just wasn't there for kids like me. My mum and dad didn't understand football or have any aspirations for me to do well in the game. Naturally, they encouraged me to always do my best, but I never had a pair of Adidas Santiago boots, for instance. My parents just bought me what they could afford.

Most kids, as they grow, need bigger boots every three months or so. My parents couldn't afford that, so I used to go on squeezing my feet into the boots so they lasted five or six months. As I grew older, I liked tight boots for that reason. I soaked them in warm water to stretch them, but over time it started to affect my feet and now I am paying the price. My feet are a size 10 in shoes – but with boots with studs I'm a size 9 and I've got painful corns on my feet as a result. I can tell you my feet are seriously ugly from having squeezed into tight boots for many years. As a professional, I used to give my boots to an apprentice to break them in.

Like many youngsters, I used to ruin my shoes by kicking a ball around. It broke my mum's heart and it was something I regretted – but you do these silly things as a kid and don't consider the consequences.

But some things are more serious than scuffed shoes.

Despite my even temperament, on one occasion I got into trouble with the police, totally going against one of my dad's oft-repeated mantras: "I don't want no policeman knocking on my door."

It was in the summer of 1974 and I was running around with a bunch of guys who used to go to newly vacated houses in Harlesden and Willesden during the school holiday and get money out of the gas meters. We'd break into houses and pop the meters. We didn't consider ourselves to be thieves, because we didn't steal jewellery. We'd just break into the meter for the money.

But one day we broke into a house that was occupied. We got out as quick as we could. Later two members of another gang we had joined up with, who were doing similar things over in Acton, broke into a house and got caught by the police.

The inevitable happened. They squealed and gave the police everyone's names, including mine. So there was a solemn knock on our door. It was two detectives, asking for Cyrille Regis. They took me to Acton police station and gave me a caution. I hadn't been caught in the act, so there wasn't much else they could do, but I had a stern warning.

Dad went berserk. I learned my lesson and changed my friends straight away. I realized I had let my family down and that if I carried on hanging around with these guys I could end up in jail. My dad believed in the old adage "Spare the rod and spoil the child", so we did experience a good hiding on the odd occasion when we misbehaved. This time he just went bananas at me. After that I pulled away from those boys and fortunately set off down a different road – on the right side of the law.

I would join up with a group of lads in our block called the Crawfords. They were older than me and into women, cars and music. Hanging out with them seemed a whole lot better and more grown up.

Throughout my schooldays I excelled on the sports field, but on the academic front I'd been middle of the road – I didn't stand out. "Could do better" was probably the most popular comment on my school reports. I left Cardinal Hinsley with seven CSEs. But at 16 I had a job lined up before my exam results even dropped through the letterbox.

Just three things would dominate my life for the next three years – work, hanging out with the Crawfords and football.

CHAPTER FIVE

"Get a Trade"

"So you think you're a man, eh?" asked my dad. He'd just seen me smoking a cigarette for the first time near our house. I was 16.

He had been a smoker all his life, but I had just started work. It was a rhetorical question, nothing else. There was no bawling or shouting. He was an authoritarian figure. Unlike now, older people were respected back then. Also there was quite an age difference between us kids and Dad.

Times were changing. This was a "rights of passage" issue. I was progressing into a man and Dad could see it. The money that I was literally puffing into smoke was money I had earned. It was my choice how I spent it. He could hardly complain too much, to be fair. His favourite phrase to each of us five children was "Get a trade", and I had started learning mine.

I wasn't frightened of hard work and always did all I could to earn myself some money. When I was at school I had milk and paper rounds, and I used to stack shelves at an Asian grocery shop on Church Road, close to where we lived.

I used the money to buy the components for my first ever bicycle, which I built myself. I found the frame and then bought the rest of the bits and pieces separately – wheels, brakes, handlebars and mudguards – and assembled it myself. I had no choice. As with so many other things, my mum and dad couldn't afford to buy these extras for their kids. So I made my own bike, though I'd always dreamed of owning a Raleigh Chopper, the popular children's bike in the 1970s.

Years later, when I was a professional footballer, it was the memory of the effort I had put in to build that first bike that made me give my son Robert a good telling-off. I had bought Robert a top-of-the-range mountain bike for Christmas and had spent Christmas Eve putting it together so he could see it in all its glory on Christmas morning. Naturally he was delighted with his present, but while we were on holiday that summer Robert jumped off the bike and it slammed into a tree. I was furious, because I'd never had a bike until I was 14, and even then I had to save up and scratch around to find the parts and build it myself. And here was my son just carelessly leaping off his bike and letting it smash into a tree.

It upset me because I remembered how much it had meant to me to own a bike, and Robert simply didn't realize. Even though his dad was a top footballer earning more than the average man in the street (though nothing like the huge sums footballers earn today), I didn't want him thinking that things that cost money didn't matter because Dad could afford to buy another. That wasn't the point.

It taught me a harsh lesson too. How do you teach kids to appreciate the things they have when you are on big wages and live in a four-bedroom house in a smart suburb with cars on the drive? When you're poor there's no choice. When you have money you have choices, but in either situation you need to understand the value of things.

When I was about 14 or 15, I had another summer job. It was at the same lace-making factory that Mum worked at in Park Royal, and I converted the big bobbins on machines into smaller spools for £10 a week. This was low-paid manual work and not what my dad wanted for us. "Get a trade", he told me. So that is what I did.

Before I had even sat my school exams I was already sorted. I had fancied working in electronics and had wanted a job working for British Telecom (BT) but instead I went along for an interview with electrical contractors Duncan & Watson, who were based in Cricklewood, and they offered me an apprenticeship even before I passed my exams. I was paid 32.5p an hour and my first take-home pay packet was £13.

My apprenticeship lasted three years, from 1974 to 1977, before I eventually got my "B" Grade City & Guilds qualification. In the first year I did a three-month block release at Harrow Technology College to learn theory, and in my second year I studied at City and East London College in Old Street.

In between, I worked on building sites, which was OK if you were working indoors but harder if you were outdoors all winter in the wind and rain. I can remember working at Fulham Hospital, Brent Cross Shopping Centre and on houses near Stamford Bridge, the Chelsea FC ground. I was just one of a group of apprentices doing the same thing.

After I had been with them for nine months Duncan & Watson were bought out by another firm called Higgins & Cattle, who were based at Ladbroke Grove, and they honoured the commitment to continue with my apprenticeship.

In line with our dad's advice, we all got trades. I became an electrician. Nilla, bless her – she had been so often away from home – joined the army at 17 and later qualified as a bilingual secretary (let's face it, she'd had plenty of practice at home!). Imbert worked in electronics. David became a gas fitter before eventually following me into professional football, and my younger sister Denise developed her mum's skills and became a pattern cutter in the fashion industry.

But this was about more than merely "getting a trade". It was about economic freedom. Having a skill meant we could potentially earn decent money throughout our entire working lives. Crucially it meant we could contribute to the family income. Within a short period of time my mum and dad's three oldest kids, Nilla, Imbert and I, were all earning and not on their "wage bill" any more.

Ironically, by the time I had passed my City & Guilds "B" Grade electrician's exams at East London College and completed my apprenticeship, I had become a professional footballer, so I never got the chance to put the skills I had spent three years honing into action. But all through that time my dad's words echoed inside my head: "Get a trade."

Getting that apprenticeship was the main focus of my life. In theory it could provide me with the skills to work anywhere around the world. A lot rested on the effort I put in. If I didn't pass my exams I could lose my job and end up labouring like my dad for the rest of my days.

I had three main things in my life. Work always came first. Second, if pushed, was my social life. Then, third, was football, although that was to gradually change.

After I got into trouble with the police I dropped that particular set of mates and started hanging around with the Crawfords. There were 13 of them and they were mainly older than me. The dad was called Master Herbie and his wife was Miss Good.

My closest friends in the family and their wider circle were Astor, Robin and Michael Crawford, who were nearest to me in age, and Steven James and Danny Johnson – that was our crew. The two other guys I hung around with were Douglas Gordon, who was slightly younger than me and sadly died in a car crash in the early 1980s, and Fitzroy Roberts, who is my nephew Jason Roberts's uncle on his father's side.

We were into cars, late nights and girls. They were proper lads. We travelled around too. Astor had an orange and black Ford Cortina Mark 1, and we'd go all over London to clubs like The Tavistock, Kingfishers, Constantine and All Nations, to a club in High Wycombe and to the Railway Hotel in Harrow, which had been made famous by The Who – it was one of the venues they played regularly early in their career.

We went further afield too – sometimes by car, sometimes on coach trips organized by the African-Caribbean community from places like Brixton or Stonebridge. We'd go to Barry Island in South Wales, Manchester or the seaside somewhere. We'd spend the day on the beach and maybe end up in a night club.

It was the days of big heavy bass sound systems competing against each other. Astor had a sound system and we were all heavily into reggae. My favourite artists were U Roy, I Roy, Dennis Brown, Bob Marley and Augustus Pablo. We used to carry speaker boxes the size of wardrobes – lugging the cases of equipment up and down stairs to the flats at Stonebridge to and from blues parties. I would often be out all night, sometimes getting home at 3am and then going straight to work.

Those were great days. It is why I'm a reggae man even now. My former West Brom team-mate Brendon Batson still calls me Reggae. I loved the baseline, drinking Special Brew and smoking – and, before you ask, it was mainly the legal stuff. I hate losing control. Even when I became a heavy drinker in my days as a professional footballer, I would never get blind drunk. I never woke up thinking, "What did I do yesterday?" It was always merry, having-a-laugh drunk. I hate seeing people falling over completely drunk, wanting to fight anyone and everyone in sight.

It wasn't just reggae. I loved the variety of music around in the 1970s. Working on a building site you had the radio on all day. I'd listen to all the music of that time, including Marc Bolan, Gary Glitter and David Bowie. I also liked the Temptations and James Brown – the sort of music that's in the background as you pluck up the courage to ask girls to dance with you.

The Crawfords were part of that. Their dad held a domino club at their house, so everyone congregated there. They would put four tables together in the front room of their house and sell booze in the corner. Guys would come to their house from all over London just to play dominoes, drink and chat. It was good fun. But I always got up for work and football. Whatever we'd been up to, I always got up the following day to go to work. And I always honoured my commitment to be up in time to play football.

My mum once taught me a valuable lesson about time-keeping. I got in late one night, probably between 1 and 2 in the morning. Mum usually woke me up at 6am, but on this occasion she let me sleep through. I woke with a start at 10am and tried to blame her: "How come you never woke me up?" She replied: "It is not my job. That is *your* responsibility."

The upshot was that I got a verbal warning from work for being late. They had what is now frequently called a "traffic light" system: you got a verbal warning, then a written warning, and if you didn't heed those warnings you were given the sack. After that particular morning I never asked anyone to wake me up again. It didn't matter if I went out and had a skinful, it was my responsibility to get up.

Hanging out with the Crawfords in my late teens was an important part of growing up – the transition to being an adult. We still meet up once a year, either in the Midlands where I now live, or in London where most of the guys are still based. When we meet it seems just like yesterday. No deference is shown towards me because I became an international footballer, it is just great fun as we hark back to our formative years. Those days were fantastic. In lots of ways, despite what happened to me later on, it was the most exciting time of my life. I discovered where I fitted in. It was full of laughs and bravado.

Away from work and Crawfords, football was the other big thing in my life. Every Sunday morning I played for Ryder Brent Valley, which was run by Tom Dolan, the dad of a school mate of mine, Neil Dolan. Tom worked for Ryder Rentals, who sponsored us and bought us a smart yellow kit. We also got a van to travel around in. We would play in five-a-side competitions and as a Sunday team played in youth leagues, including the Regent's Park League.

If you mention Regent's Park to most people they tend to think of London Zoo and amusements, but it is also a thriving place where people play sport on typical park pitches. We entered the league and stood out a bit with our sponsored kit and transport arrangements. If we were late, which we frequently were, we'd get changed in the van and just run out on to the pitch, usually to the amazement of our opposition. I played an entire season for Ryder Brent Valley in 1974–75 before I was spotted by John Sullivan, the chairman of Molesey FC, in September 1975.

A playing career was completely out of my mind. At 17 I thought I had missed the boat. I wasn't bothered, because I hardly ever watched football – certainly not live. I recall one occasion at Ryder Brent Valley when we went to watch Tottenham. It was my first big match and I remember the buzz of the crowd. Martin Chivers and Alan Gilzean were the Spurs forwards and Ralph Coates played in midfield. I loved the name Tottenham Hotspur – it sounded traditional – and, if I had a team at all, it was Tottenham I supported back then. It was a great experience but I never went back on a regular basis.

I also remember sneaking into QPR a few times with a mate from school called Tony Hogan, but I couldn't afford to go to football matches. I reckon I only ever saw maybe half a dozen matches before I joined West Brom. It wasn't part of our culture.

I loved playing football. Now, at the age of 52, I still enjoy it. Even when I was going out drinking with mates I always loved playing football. If I'd agreed to play I'd turn up. If I say yes I mean yes. I don't like to let people down and that was true of football. I'd always turn up rather than let the boys down, even if I'd been out drinking the night before and felt the worse for wear.

Everything began to change when John Sullivan came along to see me play. John is a rather colourful character with a background in the music industry as an agent, manager, music publisher and record producer. He claims to have brought early-1970s band Marmalade down from Scotland, and to have turned down a 50 per cent stake in Procol Harum and Fleetwood Mac on points of principle. He also owned a building company.

John also liked his football. He was chairman and manager of Molesey FC, who played in the Athenian League, and had bold plans to turn the Surrey club into a full-time professional outfit.

One day he received a call from a man called Bert Fiddler, who tipped John off about a few good players at Ryder Brent Valley. My team-mate John O'Riordan had been turned down by Chelsea, and Bert suggested he would be a good player for Molesey. Brent Valley had a couple of other decent players too, including a powerful centre-forward who had scored a few goals. So John came along to see us play.

John now says he couldn't believe what he saw. That I stood out and that it was like a football version of *The X Factor*. I was the football equivalent of Susan Boyle, the Scottish lady who had viewers and the judges asking where she had been hiding – except that John likened me to an Adonis who had it all!

At the end of the game, John went up to Tom Dolan and asked if I and two other players, Philip Webster and John O'Riordan, could go on trial at Molesey. Tom agreed.

John didn't waste any time plonking me into Molesey's first team. I had been playing against Under-18s and I was immediately pitched in against grown men. He spotted me on the Sunday and I was playing for the first team in the Premier

Midweek Floodlit League a couple of days later, because they could sign players for that league on the same day, which was less formal than most other Saturday leagues. I lined up to play against Tooting & Mitcham United FC, who were a well-established non-League side at the time and would have their best ever run in the FA Cup later that season when they reached the fourth round.

Apparently, when John informed his coach Tony Slade that I was playing, Tony remonstrated with him. He didn't think it was fair to an inexperienced 17-year-old to be put straight into the team without even meeting the rest of the lads. But John was manager and club chairman, so he overruled Tony. "I can and I am," he said. "He's playing."

He backed his judgement and I played well. We won – and John claims that scouts from QPR and West Ham United immediately phoned him to ask about me. I was in the side for the rest of the season.

It was exciting playing under floodlights for the first time and being watched by paying crowds. There weren't many players of my age around and few black kids – so the attitude was "Who is the cocky young black lad?" I wasn't cocky, but I guess that is how it looked, being picked for the first team so early on.

I was on £5 a week cash at Molesey. I was earning £20 a week at work, so it was an additional quarter of my weekly income just for playing football. I scored 27 goals for Molesey that season, and Sullivan never tried to change a thing about my game. He has always insisted that the player he saw on Regent's Park was as good as the player I was when I was scoring goals for West Brom a couple of seasons later.

I didn't view Molesey as a stepping stone to greater things. I was just enjoying playing a good level of football and being paid to play. A bit of extra cash always came in handy. I didn't make friends easily at Molesey though. It wasn't their fault, it was mine. I played football there, but socially my life was with the Crawfords. Remember at this time my electrician's job was my main focus. Socializing was my real passion. Football was an enjoyable sideline.

Molesey was also in well-heeled Surrey – an affluent part of the stockbroker belt close to places like Thames Ditton and Hampton Court. It was a world away from where I lived in Stonebridge.

John Sullivan lived in Hampstead and used to pick me up in Stonebridge, or at a tube station somewhere near where I had been working, in one of his fancy cars. He had a gold-coloured Pontiac Firebird and a souped-up Alfa Romeo which, as you can imagine, stood out a mile in Stonebridge.

He was always in a hurry, and we used to fly down to Molesey at breakneck speed. We would race past Kew Gardens and Richmond, and I recall we nearly crashed on Hangar Lane on one occasion. On the way back I would invariably fall asleep.

Sometimes John popped into our flat for a cuppa. We had some fascinating conversations on the way back and forth to Surrey, John liking what he called my "quiet demure". I am not so sure about that, but with his background in the music biz, John had an eye for spotting talent and he must have known that, in me, he had someone who would be valuable to Molesey.

John was a proper impresario and later revealed to me that he had harboured plans to become a football agent (long before players had agents, I hasten to add) and make me his first client. He would market me solely as "Regis", a bit like Pele. He felt I should have been the most marketable player in the country – not just a well-known Midlands player.

I'm not so sure. John was a successful manager at Molesey, steering them into the Isthmian League when it was restructured in 1977, but I am not convinced that English football was ready for that kind of thing.

The one thing that bemused John, and many other people as I whizzed through football's ranks in my late teens, was the fact that I hadn't been signed already – though he thought he knew why it was. Unlike many other people, John is unequivocal.

"No one was prepared to put their money down to sign black players," says John, who also recalls that he had to clamber out of the dugout to remonstrate with supporters who were using racist language. I have to say that I didn't hear of this myself, but John claims he shielded me from a lot of it and insists he copped a lot of personal flak. He even says he was told he was "the cause of all this trouble".

I was oblivious to all this. But hanging on to me or getting a fee for me was proving difficult. One incident which upset John was when two guys tried to tap me up. I was young and naïve and didn't know what I was doing. They wanted me to go to Boreham Wood, who played at a higher level in the Isthmian League. They showed me around the club and I was instantly impressed. The pitch was better than Molesey's, so I understandably wanted to move there.

But, as I thought, I was under contract, so I stayed put until Ian Bath, a goalkeeper who joined Molesey from Hayes, mentioned my name to the manager at his former club, Bobby Gibbs, realizing that it would be a step up for me. Both Gibbs and Bobby Ross, Hayes's assistant player/manager, who was soon to take over as manager, came to see me in action.

Ross, a tough-tackling Scotsman who had a 20-year playing career with Hearts, Shrewsbury Town, Brentford and Cambridge United before joining Hayes (and would subsequently spend a further 29 years as a youth coach), identified my skills and strengths straight away.

"A good two-footed player, with strength, power and ability with his socks rolled down and a natural attacker," recalled Bobby. "I thought if I can get him to play upfront – in the final third where you always want your best players to be so they do the most damage to the opposition – then he could be a great player for Hayes."

We chatted at length after the game, and Bobby kindly offered me a lift home as he lived in West London. As I had not signed a professional contract at Molesey as I thought, Hayes were able to sign me without paying a fee.

I knew that if I shone at Hayes I stood a reasonable chance of becoming a full-time professional in the Football League. Until this point football had been purely about fun. Now there was more purpose to it. I moved to Hayes in the summer of 1976 and was initially on £13 a week – on top of earning £30 to £40 as an apprentice electrician. Hayes, in Middlesex, was also closer to Stonebridge, so it was handier for me too. The step up from the Athenian League to the Isthmian League wasn't massive – but matches were far more competitive.

Throughout my non-League playing days my employers

Higgins & Cattle were great to me. Site foremen would always let me leave early, no matter where I was working in London, because they wanted me to do well. If I'd started having time off the next morning it might have been a problem, but because they were so good to me there was never any danger that I would abuse the trust they'd shown in me.

There are literally thousands of footballers in this country who have similarly good employers, folks who show flexibility and routinely allow them to get off work early. We should take our hats off to them.

I made an instant impact at Hayes. One of my former colleagues, Alan Carrington, who played right-back, says my talent stood out a mile. My team-mates were surprised at how big and fast I was, and Alan recalled that in pre-season training I was so quick over 50-yard shuttle runs they had to put me back 10 yards to give the other lads a chance.

Not everyone was happy to see me at Hayes. I replaced a club stalwart up front called Peter Lavers, which must have been hard on him.

In a pre-season friendly against Southall, I played against Alan Devonshire, who stood out by some distance, and I wasn't surprised to hear of his move to West Ham soon afterwards and rapid progression into their first team. Little did I know that the next time we'd be on a pitch together it would be in the First Division just over 12 months later.

Hayes had some good quality players. Bobby Ross was keen to bring in a few ex-Football League men who could add guile and experience alongside some of the reliable non-League players we already had. The newcomers included Stewart Scullion, who had played over 300 games for Watford and

Sheffield United, and John Delaney, who joined from Wycombe Wanderers.

One of my team-mates was a super-fit centre-half called Reg Leather. Alan Carrington, who was a right-back but managed to play in every position including goalkeeper during his time with the club, Bobby Wiles and Dave Yerby all hailed from Enfield in North London and would pick me up in their car on the way to games and drop me back afterwards, when invariably we'd stop to scoff some chips.

They used to call me Nugget – allegedly after the manager of one of our rival clubs said "mark the nugget", meaning me. Whether that was a compliment or intended as a racist jibe I don't know, but either way the other lads picked up on it affectionately. I didn't doubt their respect for me as a fellow player.

I had a good season at Hayes, scoring 25 goals in 61 appearances, and was the club's player of the year. My memory of matches isn't great, but I chatted through some of the games recently with Alan Carrington, and I do remember scoring both goals when we beat Enfield 2–0. Enfield were a big non-League club at the time. They had a brute of a centre-half called Brian Wilson, an imposing character who was also a cab driver. But although he tried to give me a hard time I got the better of him. I also scored four goals in a Middlesex Senior Cup Replay against Hounslow.

Alan remembers a match at Dagenham when they wound me up and I lost my temper but still turned in a brilliant performance. Bobby Ross recalls it was after this game that West Brom chief scout Ronnie Allen decided to put in a bid for me. I'd impressed him by scoring a goal in which not only the ball but also a couple of their defenders ended up in the net.

Some of the Hayes lads actually tried to bring out the devil in me. "Get him to lose his temper," they used to say, because they knew I would play in a more rugged, aggressive way. Some of the opposition took the a different stance. "Don't wind him up," I heard one team say.

I remember us driving past Stamford Bridge after one match and someone said, "You'll be playing there soon, Cyrille." A year later I did – and I scored. "You were the best up-and-coming player I ever saw by a mile – I'm amazed you got through the entire season without a club coming in for you," said Alan Carrington. That is some statement bearing in mind that Les Ferdinand replaced me at Hayes and moved to QPR a year later. Bobby Ross was lucky – he had two future England centre-forwards play for him in consecutive seasons.

Throughout that season, there were growing rumours about scouts watching me and clubs preparing to put bids on the table. Scouts certainly started looking at me from quite early on in the campaign. I remember a scout from Arsenal coming along and telling me to practise kicking a ball against a wall to improve. I thought, "Yeah, right." I was getting far better at what I was doing – learning from the school of hard knocks at semi-pro level, enjoying life and working hard to build a career either as a footballer or an electrician. I was used to playing 20-a-side games in what we called The Cage – a concrete pitch surrounded by wire fencing in Stonebridge.

Quite a few clubs, including QPR, Watford, Chelsea and Arsenal, made enquiries about me, some offering to take me on trial for a week or so. Bobby Ross had a meeting with the Hayes chairman, Derek Goodall, to discuss my future, and Bobby made it clear he didn't want me to go on trial.

"Let's make them put their money where their mouth is," he insisted. Bobby was rightly concerned that if I got injured they would lose a player and I would miss my big chance.

Another valuable piece of advice Bobby offered me was to always wear shin pads. He was a no-nonsense Scottish midfielder who knew his way around. He knew that whether they wrote it down or not, some football hard men kept what they termed "little black books", or mental notes of players they wanted to nobble.

A talented teenager wearing no shin pads could be a target for that type of player – and it was just downright dangerous anyway. He used a bit of psychology. He told me to try some pads out in training under my tracksuit bottoms so no one would notice.

Although there was speculation that Gordon Jago, the manager at Millwall, wanted to put a bid in, the London clubs sat on their hands. One rumour we heard later at West Bromwich Albion was that when I started scoring goals for fun at West Brom an Arsenal scout lost his job for having failed to tip the Gunners off about my potential.

I didn't realize it at the time, but across London the same hesitancy surrounded Laurie Cunningham at Orient. He was carving out a name for himself as an exciting winger but, yet again, the bigger London clubs dillied and dallied.

West Bromwich Albion showed no such hesitancy. Albion manager Johnny Giles took Laurie to The Hawthorns in March 1977 for £135,000, where he made an explosive start – and chief scout Ronnie Allen tabled a bid to sign me. It took a former England centre-forward to spot a future one.

According to legend he told the Baggies board that if they

didn't agree to sign me for the proposed £5,000 he would pay it with his own money and they could refund him when I made it. I don't doubt that Ronnie was Albion through and through and confident enough in his judgement to have done it, but I doubt he really did.

In those days, agents were something you only saw on *The Man from U.N.C.L.E.*, so Bobby Ross and I travelled together to The Hawthorns to sign the contract on 9 May 1977. "I wanted you to get a few extras," Bobby told me on the way there. "Maybe a car so you could travel home to see your family regularly, but I didn't want to push it too far or they would have walked away."

We got lost travelling up the M1 and M6 to the Midlands but arrived in time for me to sign. There was no car involved. Hayes got £5,000 straight away and a further £5,000 based on appearances. I was offered £60 a week plus an appearance bonus each week, free digs and a £250 signing-on fee.

I knew very little about Albion, but they were a club on the up. They had just finished eighth in the First Division and had a charismatic manager in former Leeds United midfielder Johnny Giles, although that was soon to change. No sooner had I signed on the dotted line than Giles decided to quit.

As we left the ground after I had signed, Albion's Scottish international winger Willie Johnston came over to me and asked, "Have you signed?" At the time I had no idea who he was, but I told him I had. "That's a pity," he said, "because Manchester City want to speak to you." Apparently Asa Hartford, Willie's former Scotland and West Brom pal, had asked Willie to tell me to speak to City before committing to Albion in a possible last-gasp bid to sign me. It was too late.

Chapter Five

I have fond memories of Hayes. I always got involved in off-the-field events to help the club and keep up the team spirit. Equally they got good money for me, and used it wisely by investing in new floodlights, which are still there today. In my early days at West Brom, whenever my name was mentioned the club invariably got a mention – and that helped them enormously. Scouts would turn up searching for players and it raised their profile. Les Ferdinand moved from there to QPR, and Jason Roberts, my nephew, also played for them.

Higgins & Cattle were fantastic. They let me leave with a real spring in my step. I was told that if it didn't work out I could always return to them. Ironically I completed my three-year apprenticeship in March 1977 – just two months before signing for West Brom – but I didn't have an official ceremony or an increase in wages for having passed my exams. It felt good, though, because I knew I would be more secure if the football side fell though. It was safe. I had a skill which would enable me to earn money for the rest of my life.

After signing for Albion in May, I carried on working on building sites in London until July 1977. Then, after going to Woolworths in Harlesden, buying a dark red suitcase and packing all my things in it, I caught the train to Birmingham New Street station.

When I had started my electrical apprenticeship, football had been something I merely did for fun. Now I was going to be a professional footballer. "Get a trade," said Dad. I did more than that. I got two.

CHAPTER SIX
"Hold it Up"

Not even in my wildest dreams could I have imagined that the season I was about to embark upon – my first as a professional footballer – would go so well. I would burst on to the English football scene in a dramatic and spectacular way. There would be great goals and memorable games. But there was another dynamic too. The reaction of fans to me and my fellow black team-mates Laurie Cunningham and Brendon Batson as key components in a successful team would be unprecedented and radical.

There were lots of things I was going to have to get used to in my first few months as a professional footballer. But do you know what my abiding memory of that season was? It was being constantly bawled at by Albion's midfielders whenever the ball was played up to me. "Hold it up, hold it up" was all I ever seemed to hear.

Don't get me wrong. I knew what they meant. If they were going to make lung-bursting runs forward from midfield to support the strikers, they had to feel confident that the ball wasn't going to be sent careering back over their heads, with the opposition gleefully heading the other way.

But all this was new to me. I was used to having the ball

played over the top. Then I could outstrip and out-muscle any defenders and bear down on goal. As they say in modern parlance – what's not to like about that? It would certainly thrill the crowds watching West Brom in 1977–78. But it wasn't very sophisticated – and it was very selfish. Also there isn't usually much mileage in being a one-trick pony in football or any other sport. Teams will soon suss you out and adjust their tactics.

The players shouting "Hold it up" also knew their stuff. They included Tony Brown, who netted 218 goals for Albion, mainly from midfield. For my money "Bomber" was one of the best attacking midfielders English football has ever seen, and in his day he was certainly the equivalent of Paul Scholes and Frank Lampard – only without picking up the England caps he deserved.

Then there was Bryan Robson, who would mature into the best player I ever played alongside – a future England captain who had it all. Len Cantello was a highly respected and hugely talented midfielder, while Mick Martin was a genial Irishman signed from Manchester United and John Trewick was an England youth international on his way up and a first-team squad player.

We also had the mercurial Willie Johnston on the wing, and newcomer Laurie Cunningham, one of the most silky-skilled players to grace English football. The guys playing the ball from deep included Derek Statham, a young effervescent left-back and future England player, who had broken into Albion's first team at the age of 18 midway through the previous season, and Paddy Mulligan, a knowledgeable and very experienced right-back. Then there were our ultra-reliable central defenders, John Wile and Ally Robertson, who were absolute rocks at the heart of our defence with bags of experience.

They all wanted me, and for that matter my fellow forwards, Ally Brown and David Cross, to hold the ball up – not that Ally and David, who were seasoned strikers, needed as much reminding as I did.

All this was new to me. In fact there was a lot I needed to learn about professional football. I didn't know much about West Brom before I signed for the club, or about their players. I wasn't into watching football, I was into playing the game. But it had all been free-flowing. As a young player and a new signing, of course, I expected these guys to be well off my radar in my initial period at the club – but it didn't work out that way.

There were certainly no fanfares when I got off the train at Birmingham's New Street Station. In fact, there would be few expectations or burdens placed upon me. I rather suspect that a player signed for £5,000 from a non-League club was probably of less interest to most fans than a promising England schoolboy international – if it registered a flicker of interest in their minds at all.

I was met by Ron Jukes, a part-time coach at the club, who had arranged digs for me with a black landlady he'd found via the factory in Dudley where he worked. He'd asked around to see if anyone was prepared to take in a young black kid who was moving up from London. One of the guys working there, Sydney Groce, said his mother would. The thinking was that if I stayed with a black family I would settle in easier.

So Ron drove me to home of Murtella Groce in Smethwick,

a West Midlands borough close to Albion's ground, The Hawthorns. Mrs Groce, or Sis as most people called her, is an absolute angel, and one of the loveliest people I have ever had the privilege to meet. She was so kind and loving towards me, and I have never forgotten her hospitality. Even though she is now in her 90s and living in a care home suffering from dementia, I still visit her regularly. She is a very special lady.

I was given a bedroom on the second floor of their house. This was the first time I had ever had my own bedroom. That was great – but it still felt strange becoming a professional footballer, living away from home for the first time. There were loads of quandaries swimming around my head. Will I fit in? Will I settle in? Will I miss home? Will I miss my family? Will I miss the Crawfords? Will I make new friends?

So, with a mixture of excitement and apprehension, I began training at Albion. The brief was that I would play in the reserves and the coaches would polish me into an accomplished player. Most of the time we trained at Spring Road, which was a five-minute walk from Mrs Groce's house over the canal bridge – the canal being "the cut" in Black Country dialect.

Training every day was hard work. I hadn't done full-time pre-season training before and I was wrecked. I always struggled with my stamina levels and was running around this cricket pitch at Aston University thinking, "What am I doing here?"

There was something else I had to get used to. Filling my time. Training was usually done and dusted by 12.30pm each day – I would be back at home at Mrs Groce's by 1 o'clock. Then what? I had lived such a full-on, hectic lifestyle in London that finding things to do was a problem. I soon discovered how footballers fill their time.

First we had to go through the other pre-season rituals like the obligatory photo shoots in the club's famous blue-and-white striped kit, and an open day attended by 14,000 wide-eyed fans. I sat behind a desk ready to sign autographs – though very few fans ventured down our end of the table where the reserve-teamers sat.

Most had come through the ranks including forwards Kevin Summerfield and Derek Monaghan, defenders Trevor Thomson and Brian Clarke, midfielders Vernon Hodgson, David Loveridge and Wayne Hughes, and goalkeeper Mark Grew. West Brom had a good youth development set-up at that time and had just won the FA Youth Cup. First-teamers like Bryan Robson, John Trewick and Derek Statham were recent graduates from Albion's youth ranks.

While the first team squad flew off to Alicante in Spain for a pre-season tour, I settled down with the reserves and got my bearings in Birmingham. I had only ever been to Birmingham once before – to a club called Oaklands in Handsworth, which was also pretty close to The Hawthorns.

I didn't know the area, and some of the peculiarities of the West Midlands would take a bit of getting used to. I didn't know, for instance, that when people talked about the Black Country, this wasn't a catch-all reference for the whole of the West Midlands, as I'd thought: they were referring to the industrial area to the west of Birmingham, a cluster of small towns that formed a conglomerate and was distinct from Birmingham but geographically squeezed right up next to it.

Along with Wolves, West Brom were the team of the Black Country. Most of their fans came from the Black Country, and far fewer lived in Birmingham, even though The Hawthorns bordered both Birmingham and the Black Country. Confused? I was.

Change was also afoot at Albion. Manager Johnny Giles, who had steered them to promotion a year earlier and helped to establish them as a First Division club, had quit at the end of the previous season. An often complicated character, Giles voiced dissatisfaction with the game in general but also had behind-the-scenes disagreements with the Albion board over the direction in which they appeared to want to take the club.

Chief scout Ronnie Allen, one of the club's highest ever goalscorers with bags of coaching and management experience, and the man who had spotted and signed me, had taken over as manager.

Giles had laid the foundations for the club. Following promotion, they made a good impression in that first season, finishing just outside the European places in seventh spot after ending the campaign with a flourish. Confidence was high and there were strong, experienced leaders all over the pitch. It was a good balance of youth and experience, and it was easy to fit in. You learned not to take things personally if they shouted at you. It wasn't personal – they just wanted you to get things right.

I came to the attention of the first-team guys shortly after the season started. Derek Statham, who would become a good buddy and played alongside me at Albion and England, recalls watching a training-ground friendly against Walsall at Aston

University. Derek and his first-team-mates were relaxing on a grass bank after their game and watched a left-wing cross being flung in my direction. "You hung in the air for what seemed like an age, then headed into the top corner," Derek told me recently. "We turned round to look at one another, saying, 'Who on earth is this?' You were one of the best, most naturally talented players I had seen." I scored a few goals for the reserves but my first-team call-up came out of the blue.

The evening of 31 August 1977 changed my life. There are times in life when you know you have to test yourself and that the consequences of your actions will ultimately shape who you are and what you will be. That evening was one of those moments. After that night my life would never be the same again. Cyrille Regis would be a name on every Black Country football fan's lips. Within weeks the football world would know who I was and that I had the potential to succeed and to score goals.

It would also be the beginning of a love affair with Albion's fans – which I'm pleased to say continues to this day – who probably hadn't even heard of this raw black kid signed for £5,000 from a West London non-League club.

I only found out I was playing on the day. We'd been rocked by injuries to several players – including Tony Brown, Ally Brown and David Cross – so Ronnie decided to give me a chance. I didn't really know the first-team guys, because I had been training with the reserves. We trained that morning, and at the end of the session Ronnie came up to me and said: "Go home and get some rest, because you're playing tonight!"

I went home and tried to relax but it was impossible. I was too excited. Two months earlier I had been working on a building site, and I'd been in the Midlands a little more than a month. Now I was going to make my first-team debut. I called my mum and dad to let them know I was playing and walked the mile or so to the ground that night. How many players do that at Premier League clubs today, do you reckon? When I got to the ground my new team-mates wished me well.

I remember stripping off in the dressing-room with all these guys. They didn't know me and I didn't really know them. You have to earn the respect of your peers. This was mixing it with the big boys. I remember we had a TV in the corner. Willie Johnston was joking and reading a newspaper. He was always the last to strip off and get changed.

I was too busy thinking "I have never experienced anything like this before" to focus on anything else. It was a mixture of excitement and apprehension. You start to question yourself: Am I good enough for this? How will I do? Playing a few reserve-team games and scoring a couple of goals is fine – but this was the big time. I knew Ronnie Allen had faith in me, and that meant a lot.

Outside, I could hear the crowd's chants getting louder and louder. The attendance was 15,000 that night – smaller than Albion's average league gates because it was an early-round tie in the League Cup. Our opponents were Rotherham United, an unfancied lower league team, but they were still full-time professionals, with their own aspirations of knocking out a First Division club who had started the season well. Our fans expected us to win and win well. And they were doubtless wondering how this untested black kid was going to fare. So I was nervous.

We jogged out for the warm-up, though not the organized kind they have today. We just did some basic stretches and went through our own familiar routines. Then it was back in for the team talk. I was playing up front with Laurie Cunningham and Willie Johnston – two of the quickest runners in English football at the time. That was one speedy forward line.

I ran out for the match thinking, "Wow – the crowd." I had only ever played in front of a few hundred people before, and this was completely different. I was taking it all in during the warm-up, trying to get used to it.

When the match kicked off, I ran around like a headless chicken. There were no tactics. I just followed my own instincts. I didn't know my team-mates, what they were capable of or what they wanted me do.

I missed a couple of good chances in the first half. But we went 2–0 up through a goal by Mick Martin and an own goal, so the fans were forgiving. At some clubs they might have got on my back, thinking: "He's missed a few chances – what's a young kid like this doing in the team? Get him off." Instead, Albion's supporters weren't just patient with me, they were encouraging.

For whatever reason, they just took to me. They could see I was trying hard on my debut and they responded to it. A crescendo of noise accompanied my every touch of the ball.

It probably says a lot about the Albion fans. Work hard and they'll respect you for it. They were hard-working Black Country people who toiled in factories and foundries. They understood effort, and although they want to be entertained and had been brought up on a diet of attacking teams down the decades, they knew what hard work was and they wanted to see you try hard. And they saw that in me.

They accepted me as one of their own. There were no boos or jeers when I missed a chance or got things wrong. It was "Bad luck", not "You're rubbish". It was a great reaction.

The moment it went completely my way was when we won a penalty in the second half. The crowd started chanting "Cyrille, Cyrille!" They were demanding that I take the penalty.

Ordinarily, this would have been out of the question. Tony Brown had been Albion's normal penalty taker for about 15 years – and he rarely missed. Tony wasn't called Bomber without reason. He used to rifle them hard and straight down the middle, and even if the goalkeeper got his hands on the ball he usually couldn't keep it out.

In Bomber's absence Willie Johnston had been handed the role but, hearing the chants, he waved his hand in my direction and said, "Go on, then." We were 2–0 up against lower league opposition, so it didn't seem that much of a gamble. A different game, a different player and a different situation, and that might not have happened. The funny thing was, I had never taken a penalty before. Not at Hayes, not at Molesey, not even for Ryder Brent Valley.

I hit it hard and high to the goalkeeper's left and scored at the Smethwick End of The Hawthorns. For me it was relief. I'd scored on my debut and my confidence soared. The tension evaporated and I could relax.

The crowd went mad. There were loads more shouts of "Cyrille, Cyrille!" and I scored another goal afterwards to make it 4–0. A cross came over, I chested it down and spanked it in from a tight angle. Yet again, the home fans went crazy and it was a fantastic feeling.

After the game, the press wanted to know all about

this unknown hero. There were photos taken of me in the communal team bath with the other players. All of the players had a big hot bath together, washing the scum off using big bars of soap chopped up by the kit manager from a massive block. We had a chat, then went for a drink. It was great getting to know the players socially.

I had never experienced this type of reaction from fans to players. I didn't have a yardstick to judge whether or not this was exceptional.

I was also blissfully unaware that in the dressing-room Ronnie Allen had a right go at Willie Johnston for letting me take the penalty. Allen reasoned that I might have missed, and it could have destroyed my confidence, having already missed a couple of sitters, and if Rotherham had gone up the other end, scored and pulled it back to 2–1 we'd have had to fight to hold on for a win. The professional scenario was for Willie to take the penalty, score and finish the match completely.

I was too busy celebrating with my new-found team-mates. After we got changed, Willie Johnston, Len Cantello, Bryan Robson, Derek Statham and I went over the road to the Hawthorns Hotel to drink and celebrate with the fans. We stayed and stayed and stayed. Eventually, at 3am, I got a taxi home, plastered.

I went home thinking: is this what professional football is all about? We used to drink after matches at Hayes, but not like this – and this was the pro game. I was expecting everything to be more reserved, a bit more "professional". Not so. This was the norm, as I was to discover. I woke up the following morning in a blur. Thankfully, there was no training that day.

The press reaction the next day was unequivocal. "King Regis is Debut Demon," read one headline. Another screamed, "Regis is the New Astle." I remember thinking, "I like this. It feels good." Comparisons with Jeff Astle, Albion's legendary centre-forward who scored the goal which won the FA Cup in 1968 and netted 137 times for the Baggies, seemed a bit premature. I wasn't even sure yet that I would be picked for Saturday's league match at home to Middlesbrough – but ever since Astle had hung up his boots in 1974 there had been a longing among Albion fans for the powers that be to find a new hero to replace him at No. 9. For various reasons, no one had quite managed to fill Astle's boots. Joe Mayo had been a decent centre-forward for them in the Second Division, but neither he nor David Cross, who had been bought for £150,000 in 1976 and did well, had quite captured the fans' hearts.

Probably more than most clubs, Albion fans love a striker. They'd had some great front men down the years, including Ronnie Allen, Jeff Astle and Derek Kevan, who'd all fitted the mould. By the same token I was a bit different. I was black, straight from non-League and full of youthful enthusiasm.

Ronnie Allen had been quoted before the Rotherham game as saying: "The kid is going into the side 12 months before his time." Afterwards he commented: "I dare not leave him out on Saturday because the crowd will have my head."

That was it. I was in against Middlesbrough. I could picture the guys back at Hayes reading their morning newspapers and wondering what the heck I was doing taking a penalty – but I bet they were pleased. Many people probably thought it might be a flash in the pan. But I scored again, and this time it was a spectacular goal that would become my trademark.

I think there was also that feeling of "I could do that" when my story hit the headlines. "He came from non-League, was playing Sunday morning football – why couldn't I make it?" The fans related to my background. And they thought, "You know – good on him."

When I went past a defender and ran towards goal a sense of excitement built up in the ground. The first time it happened was that game against Middlesbrough.

Middlesbrough were a decent team. Graeme Souness played in the heart of midfield. David Mills and David Armstrong were good attacking forwards, and left-back Terry Cooper had been an England player and league championship medallist with Leeds United. At the heart of their defence was Stuart Boam, a tough-tackling, no-nonsense defender.

The attendance this time was slightly higher at 19,044. It was the same reaction for me again. I ran around enthusiastically and was all arms and legs. It was 1–1 when midway through the second half I picked up the ball on the halfway line, mis-controlled it but managed to flick it on and rolled the defender, then went past another defender. Boro's back line parted in front of me. I struck my shot from the edge of the penalty area and it went in. Once again the crowd went bananas.

Subconsciously, for the rest of my years at West Brom, I knew that whenever I got the ball the sound of the crowd and the expectancy level would steadily rise. It was "He's going on another of those 30 to 40-yard runs with defenders on his back again." I couldn't have dreamed of a better start.

The team I joined was full of young lads. Full-back Derek Statham, for example, said we just gelled. "We were both young lads with similar characters. We liked to work hard and play hard. There wasn't a clique. We were just a group of young men who enjoyed socializing as well as playing, and I feel those close friendships we formed during that time were reflected in the results. We all worked hard for one another and there were no prima donnas at West Brom."

That night I went out socially for the first time with Laurie Cunningham, who was also adored by Albion fans. That's when I first got to know Laurie. We went into Birmingham city centre and ended up at a nightclub called Rebecca's. Back then it wasn't such a big thing to see footballers out on the town – it was commonplace, unlike today when footballers only go to exclusive, expensive places.

Not that I was too well known yet. Laurie and I were exciting young English players, certainly – but there was something else that was different about us too. We were black.

There were very few black footballers in English football at the time. Certainly only a few at the top end of the game like Viv Anderson at Nottingham Forest, Luther Blissett at Watford (though they were still a few leagues down at this point) and Garth Crooks at Stoke. Bob Hazell and George Berry were soon to break into the first team at Wolves. But at West Brom there were two of us, and we'd both hit the ground running.

The first time we experienced taunts from the crowd was the following week at St James's Park, Newcastle, my first away game, which we won 3–0. It was a fantastic result – and we played really well. I scored again to make it four goals in my opening three matches. Laurie and Bryan Robson got the other goals to round off a comprehensive win.

But I will always remember that game for something else. Racism. Big time. It was solely from the crowd, I hasten to add, not from any rival players. There were monkey chants whenever we touched the ball. It would become commonplace over the next few seasons, but this was the first time I'd experienced it.

Part of it, I'm sure, came from the fact that Laurie and I both scored and were two black guys tearing their team apart. Newcastle had done well the previous season, but had a poor start to the 1977–78 campaign and were relegated at the end of it, and so the decline was fast. We didn't get stick from too many fans – but it was enough for us to hear it when we got the ball.

I never allowed racism to affect me personally. If you allowed it to influence your game and your thinking, they would win. I very quickly realized that the best way to fight back was to use your talent. My talent was to play football – and to score goals. And nothing hurt the racist cowards in the crowd more than seeing black guys like me scoring goals against their team and seeing their goalkeeper having to fish the ball out of the back of the net.

That was my answer. Simple, short, sweet and effective. Through this reply of consistent perseverance and performance, people's minds were changed. Later on, I got to realize the powerful impact this had on the young black British kids who didn't go to matches because of the racism they saw the likes of me, Laurie, and soon, Brendon Batson and others having to endure on TV. At the time, though, all I was bothered about was keeping my place in the team and trying to make my way in professional football. That was hard enough.

The reaction to me and Laurie ratcheted racism up another notch. This wasn't one to one, it wasn't hidden or "institutional", it was vocal – this was crowds of people having a go at us. You couldn't pretend you didn't hear it, but equally it didn't put me off. Quite the contrary – it made me try harder. It was the same for years afterwards. Focus on the game. Fight back in the best way possible – by showing them how good you are.

As for the idea of West Brom submitting a complaint to Newcastle or the Football Association about the verbal abuse, forget it. Clubs didn't think like that. I am not sure what Newcastle or the FA would have done anyway. Probably nothing.

It wasn't uniquely their fault. Today, of course, it would be a different matter, and quite rightly so. That sort of behaviour isn't tolerated. The authorities were completely caught out by it. But it did happen again and again.

It certainly didn't affect the West Brom dressing-room, which was a happy, positive place, full of laughs. We never sat down and had an intellectual discussion about the whys and wherefores of racist chanting or whatever. It was just pure support from the lads. Ronnie Allen, and later Ron Atkinson, Albion's managers during this era, just said, "Go out and play your football." What else could you do when a couple of thousand people decide to throw derogatory remarks at you? The reality was no one knew what to do.

But the newspapers were highlighting it by referring to our colour. From the moment I teamed up with Laurie at West Brom, the press always referred to the black players, the black pearls, black gold, black magic. It was a new phenomenon.

The one chant I truly hated was "Nigger, nigger – lick my boots". That chant is loaded with overtones of colonialist supremacy, slavery and subservience. It was a horrid and disgusting chant. Still I channelled my anger into my performance on the pitch. The first time I heard that one was when we played Wolves the week after the Newcastle victory. We drew 2–2. I didn't score.

The racism was back big time the following week at another derby against Birmingham City. We won the game 3–1, but I will always remember it for the words spoken by ITV's Midlands commentator Hugh Johns after I scored my goal – "All the talk about Regis isn't just talk" – and the move that inspired it.

Willie Johnston raced down the left wing and pulled the ball back to Derek Statham, who checked and then crossed with his right foot to the far post. One of Birmingham's defenders jumped early and I brought the ball down on my chest and rifled it into the corner. That was so sweet. I scored for the first time in front of West Brom's Birmingham Road End, where most of Albion's vociferous fans used to stand. It was, and still is, known as the "Brummie" Road End, and my relationship with them was always special.

The great thing about that goal was that I shaped up to go early for the ball to fool the defender, who bought the dummy, jumped early and missed the ball completely. I had tricked him and out-thought him. That slight bit of movement towards the ball from me made him think I was going for the header.

I had hit the ground running at West Brom and was having the time of my life. I also scored in a 1–1 draw at Derby, but after that Ronnie Allen decided to either rest me or put me on the subs' bench for a time while I learned to "hold it up" and bring my team-mates into play.

For a time during this period our results remained positive. We hammered Manchester United 4–0, the same scoreline that Albion had beaten them by at The Hawthorns the previous season, but after that we went through a lull, failing to score in five games on the trot and unexpectedly losing to Bury in the fourth round of the League Cup.

During this period Ronnie offered me a bit of extra advice about handling press interviews. "Always talk about your team-mates," he said, and he used to remind me to give credit to the team rather than just talk about myself as the forward who scored the goal. I say the same thing to young players I represent as an agent today. Ninety per cent of your goals are laid on by other people – so thank them. Give them credit. Be magnanimous – you are just the one at the end of the chain.

That was something I learned early on at West Brom. You get all the glory. But you also get the stick when it goes wrong. I remember chatting to Ronnie later when I was on a bad run and the papers were caning me. "You chose your position," he said. "You take the glory. You've also got to take the stick. You chose to play there, now get on with it." How right he was.

Sadly, Ronnie left Albion in December 1977. We were on a decent run when the Saudi Arabian national team came a-calling for a coach and offered Ronnie £100,000 a year. He had to go.

John Wile took temporary charge, which worked OK, but we needed a leader and someone to take us forward. I like John a lot and respected him hugely but, to the lads' amusement more than anything else, as soon as he became caretaker manager he decided to have a room to himself on away trips instead of sharing with Tony Brown.

That didn't go down too well among the boys. Then he pulled in three of us younger players – me, Bryan Robson and Derek Statham – to reprimand us about our lifestyle. He thought we needed to knuckle down, stay in more and drink less. He was absolutely right, of course. One hundred per cent. But we were young lads and he wasn't our boss. We thought, "Are you sure, John?" Lads will be lads. He was right, but we didn't heed his warning.

Realistically, John was never going to get the manager's job at Albion at that stage of his career. He was still a key player at the heart of our defence. We needed a new manager to bring the best out of those personalities on to the pitch. West Brom's board found him, and we were to enjoy the best season-and-a-half of our careers.

It was time to say hello to "big" Ron Atkinson.

CHAPTER SEVEN
"Alright, Ron?"

The first time I met Ron Atkinson, I was with Laurie Cunningham and we were coming out of the Europa Lodge, a hotel about half a mile from The Hawthorns.

"Alright, Ron?" we said as he walked into the hotel.

We were breezing past, but he ordered us back and said, "Call me Boss."

We'd heard that Ron, who was only 34 at the time, had got the manager's job at Albion, but we hadn't met him. He wanted respect from the start and rightly so. He was the man in charge – and Big Ron, as he became known, stamped his personality on the team, the club and the whole of English football from day one.

None of the West Brom players knew much about Ron. When they first saw him, some of the lads thought he looked like the detective Dan Tanna from the TV show *Vega$*. At first sight, appointing Ron didn't appear to be a particularly ambitious decision. He was young, unknown, and had only managed Cambridge United, who were a Fourth Division club. But he breezed into The Hawthorns with bags of confidence and was a great man-manager. In most industries people would question whether some of the things Ron did

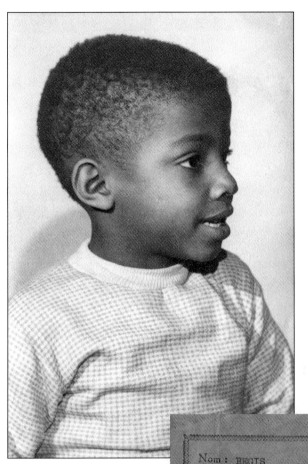

Left: An early portrait of me, aged three, when we were living in Maripasoula.

Below: I was born in French Guiana meaning I had a French identity card and passport.

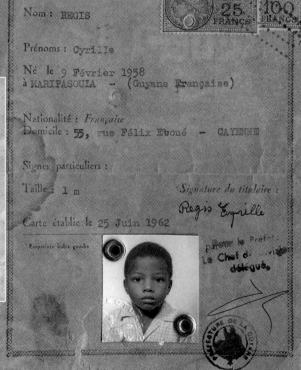

Nom : REGIS

Prénoms : Cyrille

Né le 9 Février 1958
à MARIPASOULA – (Guyane Française)

Nationalité : *Française*
Domicile : 55, rue Félix Eboué – CAYENNE

Signes particuliers :

Taille : 1 m

Signature du titulaire :
Regis Cyrille

Carte établie le 25 Juin 1962

Empreinte index gauche

RÉPUBLIQUE FRANÇAISE

Préfecture de la GUYANE

CARTE NATIONALE
D'IDENTITÉ

N° CN91747

Right: A family photo, clockwise from bottom left, David, me, Imbert, Mum, Dad and Denise.

Above: I am back row, third left, with my Cardinal Hinsley School Under-13s team-mates after the football team won two trophies.

Above: It was at Hayes where I was spotted by West Brom's Ronnie Allen. The crowds at Church Road weren't great, nor was the pitch!

Above: I get away from Chelsea's Duncan McKenzie in 1978, but Duncan was not known for his ability to tackle!

Above: Maybe I could have represented England at high-jump as well. Headers are easy when no one is marking you as in this August 1978 game for West Brom.

Above: Joe Corrigan, the Manchester City and England goalkeeper (right), may have narrowed the angle, but he still couldn't stop me scoring at Maine Road in 1978.

Above: Tottenham defender Paul Miller tries to take the ball away from me as Remi Moses (stripes) and Ricardo Villa look on.

Above: I celebrated my 21st birthday as a West Brom first-teamer. Maybe I should have sent myself a card like this.

Above: (left to right): Laurie Cunningham, Valerie Holiday, Brendon Batson, Helen Scott, me, and Sheila Ferguson, West Brom's Three Degrees and music's Three Degrees.

Above: It is always nice to receive recognition from your peers and I was delighted to receive the PFA Young Player of the Year award in 1979.

Above: Shielding the ball from Bob Hazell of QPR during the 1982 FA Cup semi-final at Highbury. A Clive Allen goal gave Rangers a 1–0 win over West Brom.

Right: This is one of my favourite photos. Taken in 1982, 18-month-old Robert looks overawed, but I'm all smiles because I have just been picked by England to make my full debut against Northern Ireland.

were acceptable, and one comment he made decades later has certainly been the subject of controversy (which I will go into later in this book), but it was all part of the rough and tumble of a football club dressing-room. Ron did everything with a laugh and joke to counteract some of the serious messages he wanted to get across.

Ron would do absolutely anything to wake you up and get you buzzing. He'd put Vicks VapoRub ointment in your face or dip your head in cold water. He would even give you a dig in the stomach to get you to tense up – just to motivate you.

When he arrived, after a promising start to the season, things had started to slide at Albion. We went through an inconsistent spell in the middle of the season and needed to dig ourselves out of it. David Cross had left to join West Ham and hadn't been replaced. That gave me a chance to get back in the side, but we didn't look like improving on the final league position of seventh the previous season.

Big Ron didn't really change the way we did things in training. It was still all five-a-sides – which had been the basis of everything at the club. Ron just wanted us to play the ball in quicker. He was keen for us to play good attacking football but didn't want us to over-elaborate. He saw that we had plenty of pace – with me, Laurie, Willie Johnston and Derek Statham – but more than anything he injected his own personality into the side.

He wanted his side to be entertaining. He wanted us to play attractive football so he would be content watching us. If he wasn't being entertained by his teams Ron wasn't happy. Ron wanted us to put on a show. "Go out there and excite me," he'd say.

After his brief spell as caretaker manager John Wile
settled back into the dressing-room as captain with no
problems. It was just one of those things. As a personality
John was quieter than most. He wasn't a joker or one of
the younger boys like me, Bryan Robson, Willie Johnston
or Tony Godden. He was different – a natural leader and a
brilliant, uncompromising defender.

Ron arrived just in time for our FA Cup fourth-round tie
against Manchester United at Old Trafford. We had beaten
Blackpool comfortably 4–1 at The Hawthorns in round three
and I got on the scoresheet, which meant I had scored on my
debuts in the league, the League Cup and the FA Cup. United
were the FA Cup holders and although they weren't really a
top team in the league at the time they were still a massive
club. At Old Trafford we drew, frustratingly, having led for
much of the match thanks to a goal by Willie Johnston. United
equalized at the end of the game through a Steve Coppell shot
which squirmed past our goalkeeper, Tony Godden.

Back at our place we beat them 3–2 after extra time.
It was a classic. We led twice, through Tony Brown in the
first half and again when I poked a shot through the mud
after a Johnston shot had rattled the crossbar. Twice United
equalized, once, as in the first tie, in the last minute.

Big Ron urged us: "You've beaten them twice – now go
and do it again." In extra time I headed in the winning goal,
my second of the game, after one of Tony Brown's efforts had
struck the bar. It was a great win, a fantastic atmosphere and
it got the ball rolling for Ron.

For me, those were heady days. I loved playing in front of
crowds of up to 40,000, winning games like that and going to

legendary places like Old Trafford. Playing well, scoring, having a great time with your mates and being well paid – it was a schoolboy's dream. Just a few months earlier, I'd been getting up at 6am every morning to ply my trade on a building site.

The bandwagon rolled on. In the fifth round we won 3–2 at Derby. I scored twice again and Willie Johnston got the other goal. Bruce Rioch, Scotland's captain at the time, netted both of Derby's goals.

That set up a quarter-final tie against Brian Clough's Nottingham Forest, who were top of the First Division and went on to win the league title that season. Mick Martin put us ahead in the first half. Then, in the second half, I latched on to a long ball which Paddy Mulligan had played over the top. I ran on to it and hit it first time. I didn't catch it right, but it fizzed into the bottom right-hand corner. I liked shooting early – it didn't give goalkeepers a chance to compose themselves.

It was a remarkable victory. I don't know why I hit it first time, but I do remember thinking "Don't let anyone catch you" and I was also concentrating on the flight of the ball. I had scored in every round of the FA Cup up to that point – and people were starting to draw parallels between me and Jeff Astle, who 10 years earlier had scored in each round when Albion won the FA Cup in 1968.

Big Ron was always at ease with the media and when promoting West Brom – but he made a big mistake ahead of the semi-final against Ipswich at Highbury. He had done an interview for a midweek TV programme and was filmed going to Wembley and walking up the steps to the Royal Box with the cup. In Ron's defence he always claimed he had been told that Bobby Robson, Ipswich's manager at the time, was going to do exactly the same thing, but that didn't happen.

The lads squirmed when we saw it go out on TV. We knew that would be Bobby Robson's team talk sorted. "They think they've won it already – now go and prove them wrong." Nonetheless we were so confident going into that match. Our fans outnumbered Ipswich's. Ron had even invited former Liverpool manager Bill Shankly into the dressing-room to wish us good luck ahead of the game.

For some reason Ron left out two key players that day – Bryan Robson and Laurie Cunningham. Our team was Godden; Mulligan, Statham, Wile, Robertson; Johnston, Trewick, Martin, Tony Brown; Regis, Ally Brown. Sub: Cunningham.

We lost 3–1. I think the worst thing about the defeat was that we didn't give a good account of ourselves. It would have been easier to take if we had played well and lost, but we just didn't play and that was terrible.

It was a huge disappointment, for the fans and for us. Back then, even if Albion drew away our coach was quiet on the way back home. A draw was like a defeat to us. If we lost, it was deadly quiet. We played to win and we expected to win every game. Those were the high standards we had set ourselves. In our hearts and minds we knew we were good enough to win that game and we had worked hard to reach the semi-finals.

Watching all the coaches pulling away with the West Brom fans slumped in their seats and staring into space was painful. It was such a big contrast to the journey down, when everything looked a huge party on the motorway.

I would have good and bad times in the FA Cup. But at that time we were a young team and we thought our day would come. We had a good balance – we had lots of good young players and bags of experience – which would become even more evident the following season. West Brom were on the brink of something special. Johnny Giles had prepared the basis for that side. Ronnie Allen carried it on. Big Ron took it to another level.

However, I don't think Ron gave enough credit to Giles for the strong foundations he'd laid. Most of the players Ron had at that time had been at the club when Johnny Giles was manager. They loved and respected the guy and what he had brought to the club. He had brought players like Derek Statham and Bryan Robson through into the first team. He had revitalized the careers of players like John Wile, Ally Brown, Tony Brown, Ally Robertson, Len Cantello and John Osborne, who had appeared to be fading. Some of his signings had proved inspirational – in particular Laurie Cunningham for £135,000, while Paddy Mulligan, Mick Martin, Tony Gooden and I had all been bought for next to nothing.

Giles had revolutionized the way the club played and the way we trained. It was his philosophy one hundred per cent. Big Ron added flamboyance and flair, pace and expression.

He could get his message across in different ways too. On one occasion Derek Statham was seen at Liberty's, a popular nightclub on Hagley Road in Birmingham, on a Thursday night. That was crossing the line. Players weren't supposed to go out drinking on Thursdays ahead of a Saturday match, and if we did go out, we didn't drink alcohol. Albion's assistant manager Mick Brown turned up and Derek, who was standing at the bar, sent over a bottle of champagne before leaving quickly.

The next day at training Ron went mad: "Derek has let you down as a team," he raged, "and if you don't beat Liverpool on Saturday I'm going to fine him two weeks' wages." That wasn't fair, we said. Liverpool were the top team in the country at the time. "You can't expect us to beat them to save Derek. Fine him now." But Ron used it to get a result. We went out on Saturday and won the game for Derek. He still got fined, but less than expected. He had learned his lesson and Albion notched up a rare victory over England's top team. That, in my book, is clever management. Big Ron turned a negative into a positive. And that was typical of him.

There was something else about Ron. He was a terrific publicist for the club. He knew all the press guys and would have a drink with them at Europa Lodge or in his office and feed them little snippets and stories to make sure we were always in the papers. He knew how to get on the right side of the press, and he worked hard to nurture those relationships. Reporters like Bob Downing, Ken Lawrence, Dave Harrison, Ralph Ellis, Alistair Ross, Martin Swain and Ray Matts used to come to games with us on the coach. When we were out we would sometimes see them and have a few drinks together. It wasn't the "them and us" situation it so often seems to be today. There was a much closer relationship between players and the sports press. They reported solely on football and didn't care what happened off the pitch.

The club was on the up. We had exciting players who were playing well and we had a manager who promoted us that little bit more. We started to get more column inches in the papers than we possibly deserved. Ron made that happen.

He was a great motivator. In training, we just did five-a-sides – he always thought he was the best player on the pitch, of course – mixed with a bit of crossing and shooting and some sprints and abdominal workouts. It was always fun.

If we'd been out drinking and had a skinful, we would put a bin-liner straight on to our skin which would help us to sweat more in order to get the alcohol out of our system faster. Sometimes you could smell the alcohol as we lined up. Ron would lock into that and give us a tough session.

The main drinking night was Saturday night. We'd get back from an away game, get off the team coach and either go straight out on the town or nip home, then go out. For a time we wore club suits, and there was no way any of us were wearing them on a night out, so then we'd nip home and get changed first.

We used to go to all the clubs in and around Birmingham – Rebecca's, Mr Moons, Barbarellas, The Opposite Lock, The Belfry, Chaplins, Hawkins, Maximillians and Snobs – and any number of pubs. You name a pub in Brum, and the chances are we had a good time in it.

We would either go out in taxis or drive. I didn't get my first car until I passed my driving test in 1979. It was a brown Austin Allegro which was a sponsored car given to me by a Ford dealership in West Bromwich.

Big Ron liked a night out and a few beers himself. He wouldn't go out with us, but if he happened to be there he would buy us a drink or a bottle of champagne. He was cool about us going out, as he was confident that we would perform on match-day.

Drinking was part of football back then. There was always a bottle of brandy or Scotch in the dressing-room at all the clubs I played for. We'd have a drink before we went on to the pitch – just a tot to warm ourselves up on cold days.

The important thing was self-discipline – and knowing your limits. If you couldn't go out and still play well on a Saturday, then don't go out. If you could go out and still play well, go out. Some players like Tony Brown and John Wile didn't go out much. They were older and wiser. They were married men and their personalities were different. They were more reserved characters.

But we had lots of younger players who thought they were impervious to it all. We were young – some single, some married – and looked good (though it is surprising how much better-looking you are when you've got fame and money!). For us, it was all about working hard in training and on match-day and playing hard off the pitch.

We finished the season strongly and earned sixth spot – which meant we had secured a place in the UEFA Cup for the following season. Although losing the FA Cup semi-final was very disappointing, I had scored 18 goals in all competitions and played 42 league and cup matches. Not bad considering that at the start of the season Ronnie Allen hadn't expected me to play in the first team at all.

At the end of the 1977–78 season I had a big and difficult decision to make. I was offered the chance to join St Etienne in France. With details of my childhood in French Guiana becoming public, a French lawyer called Christian Durancie got in touch, and that led to a clandestine meeting with St Etienne's management. The idea was that I would play for St Etienne and internationally for France.

There had been speculation about me playing for England

– and Albion were off on a goodwill summer tour of China in the summer of 1978. I didn't even have a passport yet – largely because I hadn't needed one and had never been out of the country since arriving in England in 1963.

St Etienne wanted to sign me for £750,000, and put me on wages of £500 a week. I had been on £60 a week at West Brom and had a room in a house in Smethwick. It was tempting, to say the least. The thought of living and playing football in France was also quite romantic. But there were complications. They still had conscription in France at the time. Had I taken up French citizenship I could easily have been conscripted into the French army, which would have scuppered the whole point of moving there.

I was also happy at West Brom. My career had taken off, I was part of a great team – and we had Laurie Cunningham at the club, who had become my best mate. So I stayed.

I've often wondered if I made the right choice. As far as playing for France was concerned, it was a case of now or never. The following season I played for England Under-21s and that ended the issue. At the time, though, it was a dilemma, and I agonized over it for ages. It was the end of my first year as a professional footballer, so it felt like a massive decision. There were no agents or advisers back then – no one I could really call on to help me make the right choice. At one point it all got a bit too much, so I stayed at the home of John Gordon, one of the Albion directors.

In the end, Albion offered me a new two-year contract for £200 a week – a considerable rise in wages. Three other factors helped me make up my mind. Firstly, I was still young. The chance to play abroad might come round again. Secondly, we had a fantastic side at West Brom and I was sure we would go on to win something. Thirdly, and decisively, John Gordon offered me £11,000 to stay.

The third point tilted it, obviously. For the first time in my life I had serious money in my bank account and employed an accountant, Daws & Co in Edgbaston, to advise me how to look after it. Suddenly, it seemed like a lot of money to have floating around. Big Ron didn't know about it. He offered me £2,500 to sign my new £200 a week contract, so I did well there, too.

Looking back, I do think it was the right decision. The wrong choice to leave West Brom would come later on.

The summer of 1978 was the end of my days in Smethwick. I could afford to buy my own house now – something which 12 months earlier had seemed unimaginable. I was also to embark on one of the most remarkable seasons of my career.

Not long after becoming Albion manager, Big Ron had returned to his former stamping-ground at Cambridge United and bought his former right-back Brendon Batson, who'd started his career at Arsenal.

Ron also gave us a controversial tagline, borrowed bizarrely from a chart-topping female American group – the Three Degrees.

CHAPTER EIGHT
The Three Degrees

If my first season in professional football went well, the 1978–79 campaign would be even more incredible. Sublime football was combined with rancid racism and, for me, rubbing shoulders with pop stars, being hailed as a role model and receiving an England Under-21 call-up – but ultimately the season ended in disappointment.

It all started in the summer with a tour of China. It was a goodwill trip arranged by the FA with Albion becoming the first English club to play in the country. China was still a closed country, in the grip of the Maoist regime, and they weren't used to tourists. Also, strangely for Laurie, Brendon and me, most Chinese people had never seen black people before, so when we walked past they would try to touch our hair!

We played against some local combined teams and took on the Chinese national side in the national stadium in Beijing, or Peking as it was called back then. Massive crowds turned out to watch – they would all arrive on their bikes, which was a fascinating sight – but the games were played in virtual silence as the spectators were obedient and unsure about expressing their emotions. The only time they got restless was when the famous World Cup referee Jack Taylor made a couple of contentious decisions they didn't agree with. Then an announcement was made over the Tannoy urging the crowd to please be quiet, and there was silence again.

We were also taken on cultural tours to museums and saw Chairman Mao's embalmed body in a glass case. The BBC made a documentary about the trip, presented by the well-known journalist Julian Pettifer. Some of the players enjoyed it a lot more than others. Bryan Robson was interviewed and said he would rather have gone to Alicante, but John Trewick's quick-witted joke while touring the Great Wall – "Once you've seen one wall you've seen them all" – was later misinterpreted to reinforce the "thick footballer" stereotype. That was unfair on John, who is a bright guy.

Back home, a promising season looked on the cards. Our team had the ideal balance of youth and experience – we boasted solid defenders, a range of midfield options and fast, attacking forwards. The only clouds on the horizon were doubts about whether Willie Johnston, following his drug test failure at the 1978 World Cup finals in Argentina, would be able to play for us (sadly, Willie didn't play much part in our season and after a few appearances on the subs' bench he moved out), and whether our squad would prove big enough for a tilt at the league title.

Age-wise, we had talented young players who had already amassed lots of first-team experience. I was 20, Laurie 21, Derek Statham 19, Bryan Robson 20, John Trewick 21 and goalkeeper Tony Godden 23. We had two players over 30 – John Wile and Tony Brown – but when the season started many of our players were in mid-career: Brendon Batson was 25, Ally Robertson 26, and Len Cantello and Ally Brown both 28. Early in the season Paddy Mulligan and Mick Martin moved out, along with Willie Johnston.

Albion had a fantastic blend and we were great mates together. It was the best team I ever played in, with the possible exception of the one at Aston Villa in 1992–93. We should have won the title that season, but instead were left with memories of playing great football, classic matches and "precious moments" of inspiration.

Our first goal was scored in the opening minute of the season in the 2–1 win against Ipswich and we finished our league campaign, unusually back then, after the FA Cup final, because so many games had been postponed during the midwinter freeze. The "winter of discontent" not only signalled the end of the outgoing Labour government but also put paid to our chances of winning the First Division championship.

During that season Ron Atkinson – who wasn't slow to spot a media opportunity – described Brendon, Laurie and me as the Three Degrees. The moniker stuck and led to us meeting and socializing with the real Three Degrees singing group when they came to perform at a popular entertainment venue in central Birmingham called The Night Out. As part of an amazing PR stunt they also watched us play at The Hawthorns.

Sadly the racist stick that Laurie and I initially copped the previous season had got worse since Brendon had joined West Brom in March 1978. Three black players in one team was just too much for some supporters, whose monkey chanting had even stretched to bringing bananas to hurl on to the pitch. Nothing was being done by clubs, police or the football authorities to curb this behaviour which had, frankly, been going on far too long to be dismissed as a passing fad.

The racism spread to most grounds after Brendon came on board. West Brom were doing well, so we were now high-profile players. Almost everywhere we went we got racist abuse to one degree or another.

Arguably we hadn't done ourselves any favours by being filmed together – thus apparently separate from West Brom's white players – during the China trip. Also, in a pre-Christmas photoshoot we wore Santa outfits, and the picture was subsequently run beneath the headline "Look Who's Dreaming of a White Christmas." It was cringeworthy stuff.

"The racism was nothing new to us – it was the volume," recalls Brendon. "We knew the grounds where we'd get abuse and bananas thrown at us – mostly in London and up north. But it was a great motivator. We just puffed out our chests and got on with it."

After we'd won 3–1 at Chelsea we showed the scowling home fans the score with our fingers. "We'd be hauled in front of the FA for that these days," laughed Brendon, when I spoke to him about it recently. "I was pleased they had fences up at Stamford Bridge, to be honest. We just said to the people who gave us stick, 'See you next week, next month, next year – we're not going away'."

That summed up the attitude of Brendon, Laurie and me. We weren't going to let them put us off playing – and it didn't affect our style either. "We played with a smile and made a lot of people happy," said Brendon, who also paid tribute to the fantastic temperaments we needed to ignore the abuse. "You hardly ever got booked. You took the knocks but always got back up again."

The grounds that really stuck out were Leeds, West Ham, Birmingham, Everton, Tottenham and Chelsea. At Spurs they used to sing: "Who's that up a tree – Big Cyrille, Big Cyrille."

There was always the monkey chant. It is captured best, and you can still hear it, in Granada TV's coverage of the famous 5–3 victory over Manchester United at Old Trafford – which I will come to – when Laurie picks up the ball before setting up our first goal. For once, a commentator, Gerald Sinstadt, had the guts to comment on what was going on when he referred to "the booing of the black player".

Most commentators and newspaper journalists simply ignored it – hoping no doubt, and with the best of intentions, that if the racist jeers weren't mentioned, the idiots doing this kind of thing wouldn't be given any attention and it would wither away.

But how can you fail to notice bananas being thrown on to the pitch? No one can tell me that this wasn't calculated and thought out by the perpetrators. How many people do you know who casually take fruit to a football match and then just happen to get so carried away with racist chanting on the day that they hurl it on to the pitch? Of course not – it was all premeditated. These people knew precisely what they were doing. They were trying to demean Brendon, Laurie and me as people, let alone as sportsmen.

We used to get abusive letters through the post too. Laurie copped it worse because he went out with a white lady, Nikki. Brendon was married to a black lady, Cecile, and I eventually married Beverley, who is also black.

We got very few comments from rival players, though. I was only ever racially abused on the pitch twice. Once was in the First Division by a player who was old enough to know better and well past his sell-by date. He wanted a reaction but I just laughed at him and got on with my football.

The other incident was when I was 38 and a 20-year-old called me a black bastard. "Are you for real?" I said. "I've played for England. You're only 20 – what have you achieved? The only reason we're on the same pitch is because I'm 38. If I was your age we wouldn't be playing against other because we'd be leagues apart."

None of the racism ever came from Albion fans – or those of any of the other clubs I played for. I think that helps to put things in context. In my opinion, by behaving in this way the bigots only demonstrated their ignorance and lack of character. When someone feels the need to chant songs like "Nigger, nigger, lick my boots" it reflects more on them than it does on us. Nonetheless, it was shocking that in the 1970s and 80s such overt racism was displayed for the world to see.

I believe that deep down, every human being knows we are born equal. The colour of your skin or where you may have been born can certainly create a disadvantage. However, there are numerous examples of people overcoming the odds of prejudice, subjugation and injustice, for example Nelson Mandela, Martin Luther King and even many of the first generation of men and women coming to the UK from the Caribbean. Instinctively as human beings we're on an equal footing. To judge someone by the colour of their skin shows fear and insecurity about who you are.

Thank God we knew who we were. Our character was being hugely tested. What if we had reacted differently? Just imagine if players like me, Laurie, Brendon, Garth Crooks, Viv Anderson, Bob Hazell, George Berry and Luther Blissett had reacted by fighting with the crowd. A reaction from us might well have been deemed justified, but in my view that was not the answer. The same people would have said: "Look at them – they can't handle it. They've got a chip on their shoulders."

But none of us did that. It took a white Frenchman, Eric Cantona, to react to abuse from the stands in a violent way almost 20 years later.

People ask me if it was difficult to ignore the racism coming from the terraces at that time, as if you can just switch it off and put it out of your mind. Maybe I didn't see the faces of those at the back of a stand shouting, but when I went to retrieve the ball in front of the fence people would sometimes scream in your face. Of course it is personal, of course you hear it – and you are angered by it.

Equally, I also had a tool, a weapon if you like, to fight back with. I wasn't helpless – quite the opposite – because I had my talent. I used that instead. The more abuse I received, the more I channelled my anger into my performance. Some might say I should even thank those racists for propelling me to perform so well. I wouldn't go that far, but it's true that you can turn any negative situation into a positive. When people say words don't hurt, it isn't true. Words can have a devastating and long-lasting effect on a person (just ask the counsellors of people who have been abused or bullied), but you should try to take that experience and use it to make you a stronger more balanced person; not angry, just stronger.

They were there to watch football and support their club. That meant you could hurt them simply by winning the game for your team and beating theirs. In effect – and this is something these fools never realized – they were inspiring you to do the opposite of what they wanted, which was for you to cower and run away, not to go on and win the game. They made it harder for their team's players, because we had an extra incentive to win.

We were also in a good team – a group of talented players who could help you score goals. The racists may have thought we were defenceless – but we weren't. As well as our strength of character and a good grounding of values, we of course had all of our team-mates' support.

I wouldn't say racism made me a better player, but it gave me extra motivation to perform to the best of my ability, and a determination to believe: "You know what, you can chant and talk all you want, I'm the one on the pitch scoring goals and beating your team." In the end, I and the other black players were the winners.

You can't control what people say or what they think. As long as you don't allow the opinions of others to affect your vision and plans, and you remain focused and diligent towards your personal goals, in the end you become a stronger person.

The thought of being a role model for other black players didn't enter my head back then. The harsh reality is that you're just doing all you can to stay in the side – and it was hard to get into the West Brom side back then. That was my focus, just staying in the team.

History tells us that we inspired subsequent generations of black British kids, but at the time we didn't know what was going on the heads of young boys. We were dealing with what was happening in the here and now. Looking back, I can see that we were pioneers in our time, paving the way and opening the door for the diversity of players that you see in the beautiful game today, who are judged purely on their ability to play football.

Although I had a decent season – and did manage to hold down my place in the side – the main difference in 1978–79 was the rejuvenation of Ally Brown, my strike partner. I was maturing into the sort of player who could hold the ball up, but Ally, a Scotsman signed by Albion in 1971, was proving to be a deadly finisher with 23 goals in all competitions that season.

Ally was right up there among the best strikers I played with. As a partnership we were a handful, and he was an unsung hero for much of that time. People always talk about me and Laurie, but I linked up much more with Ally. Laurie played out wide – he could drift left or right, it didn't matter to him. The three in midfield simply adjusted to wherever Laurie went.

Ally was the elder statesman out of the pair of us. He knew how to make runs and we balanced each other perfectly. Defences tended to concentrate more on me, because I could run past them and hold the ball up, whereas Ally was smart in terms of timing his runs to get in on goal and picking up bits and pieces around the box. We banged in 39 goals between us that season.

In the middle part of the season Ally had a remarkable spell when he netted 19 goals in 29 games. Strangely he had been in and out of Albion's team throughout most of his career there, and it was only when Ron Atkinson arrived to boost his confidence that Ally rediscovered his touch. He was also among a small group of players at Albion who smoked – the others included me, Willie Johnston, Tony Godden and John Osborne. It wouldn't be tolerated today of course, but back then, although it was frowned upon, it was no big deal.

That season we should have won the league. We played some fantastic football. We won three on the trot at the start of the season – against Ipswich, QPR and Bolton – then drew the next four 0–0. So much for being a free-scoring team! We did discover our magic touch in front of goal, though, and we should have beaten Liverpool, who went on to clinch the title, early in the season at The Hawthorns. We led thanks to a goal from Laurie Cunningham and thought we had added a second, but it was ruled out for offside. But Liverpool were always difficult to beat, and when we were 1–0 in front Tony Godden allowed Kenny Dalglish to cheekily nip from behind him when he was rolling the ball out and Dalglish scored. We were gutted. We gave Tony some stick afterwards and, for ages, when he got the ball Tony would cling on to it for dear life and nervously looked left and right to make sure everyone was in front of him before releasing it. Tony made plenty of great saves to atone for that momentary lapse of concentration. He was a fantastic shot stopper but as he wasn't the tallest of goalkeepers, he sometimes struggled with crosses.

Once the side began to pick up momentum we started to hand out some real beatings. We hammered Coventry City 7–1 and were well worth it. We could have doubled our score that day. We went through a spell where we only lost twice in 24 games, to Liverpool and Leeds, and won most of the rest.

Goals came from all over the pitch. Ally Brown and I bagged most of them, but Tony Brown and Laurie Cunningham both got into double figures, and Bryan Robson typically weighed in with eight goals from midfield. In all competitions, four of us scored more than 15 goals each.

Tony Brown was the best attacking midfielder I ever played with. How Bomber only ever got one England cap I will never know. You look at his record – to score over 200 goals from midfield is astonishing. Today he would almost certainly have progressed by changing clubs. Players nowadays plan their careers so they play at the top clubs, and the best players will only go to clubs that compete in the Champions League. It wasn't like that in our day. If you loved the club you stayed there. I was at two clubs for seven years each. The loyalty factor was stronger then.

The main thing that made players move on then was not getting in the side. Now, once they are at a top club, players will remain there as a squad player. It didn't happen in my day. If you weren't happy at the club you put in a transfer request and moved on. Some would even drop down a league.

Tony Brown was immensely loyal to West Brom – and the best player I ever saw running on to the ball and into the box. The best. End of story. He was scarily talented. When the ball went wide he would time his runs perfectly. He was a brilliant player – and these days he adds his valuable opinion as a summarizer for Albion games on a West Midlands radio station. His enduring passion for West Brom comes through in every line.

We had a great team. Ron Atkinson used to say to us: "Have a look around the dressing-room – who would you swap?" I'm glad I had all of those players on my side.

Our season was defined by some huge games. The most glamorous ones were against Valencia in the UEFA Cup. They were big spenders in Spanish football at the time and had signed Mario Kempes, who was Argentina's top scorer when they won the 1978 World Cup, and German midfielder Rainer Bonhof, one of the best players in world football.

We drew the away leg 1–1, a game that was really all about one player, Laurie Cunningham. He was sensational. It was that performance that sold Laurie to Real Madrid at the end of the season. The Spanish press were falling over themselves to come up with superlatives to describe his performance. Everything he tried came off. He was electric. Unbelievable. There was a great atmosphere. The home fans weren't impressed by Valencia's performance, so they started chucking oranges on to the pitch. We were used to bananas!

Laurie was having a good season but was still inconsistent. People always said he was too inconsistent. I believe that if he could have been his brilliant self week in, week out he would have been the best player in the world by far. We left the pitch kicking ourselves for not winning, but we had established ourselves and done West Brom proud. I had a couple of chances which I fluffed – and typically it was Laurie who set me up both times. But we were pleased with a draw and we knew we could beat them back at The Hawthorns.

Although we were disappointed not to win, we had a great time – and our priority was to find a nightclub to celebrate. Our routine for away European matches was to leave

Birmingham on Monday morning, arrive Monday afternoon and walk around the local shops to buy some presents. There would often be some sort of tour or photo opportunity on the Tuesday, when we would also train. We would play the match on the Wednesday evening, then find a nightclub to relax – and return home the next day.

Sometimes we would leave for England at seven in the morning, having only got in at 4 or 5am. Honestly, just two hours' kip. We'd be getting our kit together while still half drunk. At times, the press would be with us. We'd always find somewhere to have a drink and enjoy a bit of banter.

We knew we could finish off Valencia at home. European nights at The Hawthorns were special. Valencia brought all their best players to the Black Country – and we hammered them. It was a cold night and the ground was packed an hour before kick-off. We knew they wouldn't fancy it and we were well up for it. Bomber got both goals. He was wonderful that night, as on so many big occasions. His second was a cracking volley from one of Laurie's crosses. Again Laurie was magnificent.

We were bang on song and full of confidence back then in 1978–79. Our away form was brilliant. We had won 3–1 at both Chelsea and Leeds United early in the season, and we sped to the top of the First Division table, winning at Ipswich and in driving rain at Bolton in November. We then won three consecutive games on our travels in December, firstly taking the Black Country derby at Wolves 3–0, then beating Arsenal and Manchester United over the festive period.

In his commentary on the Wolves game, ITV's Hugh Johns describes me using my chest as a "passing instrument" as I help Tony Brown set up our third goal for Ally Brown to score – which made us all laugh, although we knew what he meant.

If we went away and only drew that season, the coach on the way home was like a morgue. We had confidence and we expected to win. Although we respected the opposition, we knew we had the players who could beat anyone and we didn't care what formation they played because we knew we could steamroller over them.

We hit the top as 1979 began. But the weather was shocking – it was a forewarning. On New Year's Day we played Bristol City at home on snow. We had pimpled trainers specially designed for playing on artificial surfaces and ideal for this type of match. Bristol City weren't so well equipped and we tore them to pieces. They couldn't balance, whereas we were well kitted out and managed to keep our feet. A week later we went top after a draw at Norwich. I scored our goal.

One tremendous game truly showcased our team that season. It was played at Old Trafford on 30 December 1978, just two days before the Bristol City game. There had been driving rain all day, and a bus strike made it difficult for people to get to the ground, but the 45,091 people who made the considerable effort to get there were rewarded with a match that is still cherished to this day – even though most of those watching at the ground didn't necessarily appreciate the result: Manchester United 3, West Bromwich Albion 5. It was certainly the most magnificent game I ever played in, a feast of football in which United played their part but which showed off Big Ron's Albion at our very best. Luckily the TV cameras were there to record it.

We had gone into that game flying. We'd won eight and drawn two of our previous matches. We were in the zone, high on confidence, and playing with a swagger. When you are playing in a team that is buzzing, you don't think you are ever going to lose. Losing doesn't come into it.

It was a classic game that epitomized everything West Brom were about at that time. Even now when I travel around the country, people will always mention that game. It was our signature game. People will often say they supported Albion or developed an affinity for the club because of that match.

United played really well. They took the lead twice and we pegged them back. The playing surface was awful, having cut up because of the heavy rain, but we still played great football on it. In fact as Big Ron began his half-time team talk he was under the impression that we were losing 3–2, because when Tony Brown equalized to make it 3–3 on the stroke of half-time, Ron was already making his way down to the dressing-room from the directors' box, where he sometimes preferred to watch matches.

Ron started saying, "Don't worry, we can get this back" – and we were all thinking, "Where's he been? We're level."

There's no point going through the goals one after another – but I will mention the ones which stood out, such as Brian Greenhoff's volley to put United in front. It was a fantastic strike. Our first equalizer was notable mainly for Sinstadt saying in his commentary "the booing of the black player [Laurie] has paid off" – just as Laurie played Tony Brown through to score with a left-footed shot! Sadly we were booed all afternoon. It was typical of the stick Brendon, Laurie and I received from the crowd most times we played away from home.

One of the goals people remember, which illustrated our cohesion at the time, was our second, when Laurie played me in and I back-heeled it to Len Cantello, who fired a right-foot shot into the back of the United net from the edge of the box.

When I eventually scored myself I felt mainly relief. Manchester United's goalkeeper Gary Bailey had pulled off two magnificent saves to deny me – one where I hit the ball with my left foot (yes, I did say my left foot) on the half volley. It was a sweet shot and it took off like a rocket on its way towards the top left-hand corner. Bailey made a great save – and he also clung on to another effort from a similar range. In the end I did bag the final West Brom goal. Laurie picked up the ball right in the corner and sprinted 50 yards before playing in Ally Brown. Ally eyed me running into space to receive his pass and I rounded off the move by rifling the ball home.

"Oh, what a goal!" screamed Sinstadt. I was named man of the match and presented with a magnum of champagne, which we opened on the coach on the way back down the M6.

That victory at Old Trafford showed West Brom at their best and demonstrated perfectly that it is all about team effort. As a striker you might manufacture around 10 per cent of goals yourself, but the remainder are created by your team-mates. The team has to be on song to score goals – and we certainly were.

Our team at that time had cohesion, style, strength, flair, creativity and movement, which we displayed to the full on that soggy December day. Everything came together and it remains our signature game. Many people still talk about our great games in Europe, and how we could have won the title but for the big freeze of January and February 1979.

In political terms, it was also the "winter of discontent". The Tories eventually used the images of rubbish piling up in the streets, strikes and dole queues to proclaim that "Labour isn't working" on enormous billboards. Our problem was that Albion weren't playing.

Because of the freezing conditions we managed just seven games in two months – and one of those was on 1 January – and we played Leeds three times, twice in the FA Cup and once in the league at the end of February. In between, over a period of 58 days, we played four league games – and then had to play 24 matches in 10 weeks! It was far too many and took its toll on our tired legs and small squad. In short, it left us knackered.

Disappointingly we were also knocked out of the UEFA Cup at the quarter-final stage, having been favourites following our defeat of Valencia. We lost 1–0 at Red Star Belgrade in front of 95,000 fans – but fully expected to get that back at The Hawthorns. There I levelled the tie with a first-half volley, and we pummelled them in the second half, but couldn't quite get the winning goal. They were also a very physical team and we picked up lots of knocks. In the final minute Red Star made a telling breakaway. Ally Robertson, normally the most reliable player in our team, mistimed a tackle and the visitors went through to score. We were gutted to draw a game we had bossed and to lose the tie. Our European adventure was over.

Towards the end of the season we were exhausted and effectively the league title was lost at Bristol City on Easter Tuesday. Twenty-four hours earlier, our Midlands neighbours

Aston Villa had done us a big favour by beating Liverpool and that slightly held open the door for us, but we couldn't help ourselves and went down by a solitary goal at Ashton Gate. Although I certainly ran, sprinted and tried my best in that game, there was no sharpness there and it was a painful experience. Three inches of mud on the pitch didn't help our particular brand of football either. We blew it – then we drew five consecutive games after that defeat.

As the season that never seemed to end rolled on into May, we regained our true form and won the next four games against Everton, Manchester United, Southampton and Aston Villa. But the Albion rollercoaster then took another dip with defeats against Tottenham and Nottingham Forest. Amazingly, having contested the title with Liverpool for so long, we had dropped so many points that Forest caught up with us so we had to settle for third place in the table.

We just couldn't have gone out and won all those games in such a short space of time – not with the size of the squad we had. To be fair to Ron, he'd added an extra striker, David Mills, but he needed time to bed in. The momentum we'd built up before the big freeze had ebbed away, and the explosiveness we needed to win games just wasn't there any more. Believe me, we beat ourselves up about what happened that season, but to come so close when few people had given us a realistic chance was incredible. I genuinely believe that if the bad weather hadn't halted us when we were on song we would have gone on to win the title.

We were distraught to end up pot-less. The press dubbed us the nearly men. I hated that tag, because deep down we knew we were better than that. We thrilled people, we put smiles on faces and we made youngsters want to play in our trademark, free-flowing style. We certainly weren't second-rate or losers in the eyes of the public – we were winners in plenty of other ways, and I was delighted to be named the Professional Footballers' Association's young player of the season.

Sadly for West Brom, I don't think they have had a better team than the one which very nearly captured the title 30 years ago. That was the last time they were a big noise at the top of English football, so it's not surprising that their fans hark back to those halcyon days. Sure, they've had good times since with four promotions to the Premier League and couple of FA Cup semi-finals, but dreams of top-flight success seem a long way off.

It's the same for Coventry City fans, whose club have failed to reach the dizzy heights again after capturing the FA Cup in 1987. Every subsequent team is compared to that one. It is unfair – but that's the way it is. It helps drive football clubs forward.

Manchester United's players had similar baggage for decades too. Every team was compared to United's European Cup winners of 1968. It took 31 years for United players to surpass that milestone by winning the treble in 1999. The fans don't dwell on 1968 any more. It is history. Another benchmark had been laid down and the club has been taken to a new level.

The most disappointing aspect is that Albion's board failed to realize that we had something very special and needed to build on it. They should have set about creating a dynasty at The Hawthorns. After all, we were mainly young players. They should have done whatever it took to keep us together.

Like a fine wine we should have been allowed to mature – and improve with age. As it is, we'll never know how much better that team might have got with more experience, if the key figures hadn't left and players had been brought in to complement the talent we already had.

Laurie Cunningham and Len Cantello left immediately, for Real Madrid and Bolton Wanderers respectively. Tony Brown was near the end of his career and never regained his form of 1978–79. Within two seasons, Bryan Robson would also leave for Manchester United, while John Trewick headed north to Newcastle United.

Len left after his testimonial match at the end of the 1978–79 season – a game between his XI and a team selected by me – with my side made up entirely of black players. Len had been tipped to join up with Asa Hartford at Man City, who had been a good pal when they were at Albion together, but ended up at Bolton, which was a backward step in my view.

The really big loss was Laurie Cunningham. Amazingly, he wasn't offered a new contract with an improved deal. He left Albion on £120 a week. (I was on £200 a week, having been paid £60 a week just a year earlier.) This was peanuts for a player who was helping to fill the ground. I knew Laurie better than most, and I genuinely believe that if his wages had been increased there's every chance he would have stayed.

Albion had the money. They were regularly attracting more than 30,000 people through the turnstiles but, unlike today, the star players weren't reaping the rewards. Common sense told you that they should have tied Laurie up by offering him an improved deal – but that never happened. Laurie was brassed off about being on £120 a week. So, unlike me when I was tempted to join St Etienne a year earlier for considerably more money but decided to stay, Laurie left.

Albion were happy to bank the £900,000 fee they received for him. They only made Laurie an offer after Real Madrid came in. He realized that Albion were only interested in offering him more money because he wanted to leave, not because they thought he was worth it, so he thought, "Stuff it, I'm off." Yet £300 a week would have kept him.

I was gutted. Laurie was a good mate and we played well together. Although Brendon was also one of the Three Degrees, he was a bit older and more mature. Laurie and I were closer – like two peas in a pod. We went through a lot together. Laurie was only 22 when he left. A couple more seasons at Albion and I think he would have been able to handle life in Madrid a bit better.

What West Brom needed was a long-term vision. They should have looked at Manchester United in the 1950s or Liverpool in the 60s and said, "Right, that is what they have done." Albion didn't, and the results were there for all to see. If you look at Liverpool around that time they added players to their mix. They would go out and buy good youngsters, then put them in the reserves to mature and get used to the demands of the club before elevating them to the first team. Albion should have noticed that Liverpool and other forward-thinking clubs had a good nucleus of players – then added to them.

Remember we were one of the most talked-about teams in the country. We'd finished third in the Division One table but should have finished second, or even first. We could have snapped up some of the best talent in the country to join the reserves then brought them into the first team as some players got older. But it didn't happen. It is easier to add players when you are a strong team that is doing well. You're not desperate for players then. When clubs know you're down on your luck and need to bring in players because you haven't got much talent around, the fees and wage demands are higher.

Laurie's departure also sent out the wrong message to those players left behind. A feeling of uncertainty spread through the club. If Laurie was allowed to leave, then so would others. That of course is what happened, and within two years Bryan Robson was also on his way. The overwhelming message to the rest of the football world was that West Brom lacked ambition.

I don't know how our manager Ron Atkinson really felt about things. Whatever his views or whatever disagreements or misgivings he may have felt, Big Ron never transmitted them to the players. He always kept things positive.

By the time the 1979–80 season kicked off, Laurie and Len had been replaced by Gary Owen and Peter Barnes. No disrespect to those guys, but they simply weren't the players who had left. Ron also brought in striker John Deehan from our Midlands neighbours Aston Villa. Barnes was a skilful, old-fashioned winger and an England international, but without Laurie we lost the chemistry on the pitch. Gary Owen was a young England star, but with Cantello and Robson in the centre of midfield we had been a potent force. Again, we'd lost something unique.

Me? Well, I'd had to get accustomed to being a big football

name very quickly. And I am not sure I handled it well. After just two years as a professional footballer, I was famous – but who teaches you how to deal with fame? Back then, no one did. Today you see all these people who want to be famous through reality TV shows and talent contests, but with fame comes paranoia and ego. Here I was, this well-known footballer, mixing with the Three Degrees, chatting up women and enjoying a few drinks. Of course you have a bit of a swagger about you – fame gives you that – but life can teach you a harsh lesson. Unfortunately, some people fail to learn it and have to live with the consequences. I know I did.

Following a night out with the "real" Three Degrees I ended up smashing my car. The ladies came to watch us play at The Hawthorns and we moved on to a Birmingham club part-owned by Andy Gray called The Holy City Zoo. We partied there long into the night before deciding to head back to Laurie's place for a few more drinks. The group had a driver with a big black Daimler limousine. On our way to Laurie's at four or five in the morning we were following the limo along Livery Street in Birmingham city centre when I turned left and – bang. I'd had a few beers and I crashed the car. Luckily for me it was still drivable, and there were no police involved, so I wasn't breathalysed. Somehow I'd got away with it. The girls went back to London.

I was stopped about 13 times around that time but I was never breathalysed. The police would let me off when they recognized who I was. I wasn't pie-eyed drunk – just over the limit. Again, with hindsight, this was appalling behaviour – but attitudes were different 30 years ago. Drinking was a big part of the football culture.

Chapter Eight

For my first two years at Albion my closest mates were Laurie and Tony Godden. After Laurie departed for Real Madrid, I became really good mates with Derek Statham. At lunchtime after training Derek and I would meet up at a pub called The Marksman in Carters Green, West Bromwich – often just the two of us. I remember the landlord's name was Wally and we'd have something to eat and play pool. Sometimes we'd just have a pint or two and then go home.

On other occasions there would be a few of us and anything could happen – we might not get home till 5 or 6pm. There was a pub in Birmingham called The Odd Spot that stayed open all afternoon. So if we fancied a session after Wally's, that's where we'd go. There would be loads of professional people in there – and a few villains. It was open between 2 and 7pm, when most pubs were shut. If we didn't go there, we'd go for a drink at the Revue Bar, a strip joint in Handsworth. Anywhere, basically. It wasn't a healthy lifestyle.

Later, in the mid-1980s, starting at West Brom and carrying on into my time at Coventry, I would go out drinking on Sunday too. Sometimes after a big night out drinking on a Saturday night, we'd be back in the pub at 1pm, and anything might happen from there. We knew a few places that would stay open all afternoon and carry on drinking.

We were young, so our bodies could cope. Training largely comprised five-a-side games. You didn't have hours of tough technical coaching or biomechanical or physiological testing as they do today.

Off the field, my personal life changed. The experience of fame and money meant I gave way to sexual temptations which were irresistible to a young man. I do know that when you're a footballer, famous and wealthy, fame can be dangerous, you never know why someone likes you. But then I was only 20 and wasn't in the business of tying the emotional in with the physical.

Laurie and I spent lots of time together – but we weren't always in the pub. Beverley, who became my first wife, worked at the Lilac Tree restaurant in Rackhams, a department store in Birmingham city centre. I fancied her right from the start. Beverley had a friend called Pauline who caught Laurie's eye, and we used to bump into them because we'd go shopping to fill some time and hang out there.

Beverley and I started going out in March 1978. There were some one-night stands in between – it was very easy for me to pull women. You still had to have a chat-up line, but it is much easier when you're famous – and as I've said, it's surprising how good-looking you become when people know you've got money.

Living on the edge of discovery was also part of the buzz. You know you are adored by thousands of fans and it adds to the excitement. I didn't care about whether the women I slept with loved me. Beverley was different, but I still cheated on her. It is something I bitterly regret and years later led to inevitable consequences.

In 1979, two years after being pleased as punch just to have my own bedroom, I bought my first house. I bought it from Bryan Robson, who in turn had got it from Len Cantello. It was 53 Beechglade, Handsworth Wood, and it cost me £24,000.

I asked Beverley to live with me. It was hardly a romantic proposal. I was coming round after being dosed up with morphine for my cartilage operation.

CHAPTER NINE
Three Lions on my Shirt

Albion made a dreadful start to the 1979–80 season – and it started badly for me too. I got injured in a home friendly against China, which was a return fixture following our trip the previous summer. I remember the goalkeeper slamming into my right leg. I was in agony. It was my first major injury – requiring a cartilage operation – and rotten timing. West Brom won just one game in the opening two-and-a-half months. I was out of action and, all in all, it was a miserable time.

A real period of transition was beginning at The Hawthorns. We'd lost Laurie Cunningham and Len Cantello to Real Madrid and Bolton respectively. New faces Peter Barnes, Gary Owen, David Mills and John Deehan were all bedding in to the side, and Gary Pendry had joined from nearby Birmingham City as cover for our left-back and my good pal Derek Statham. Pendry ended up playing more games than he'd probably hoped for, as Derek missed most of the second half of the season.

The club's goalscoring legend Tony "Bomber" Brown hardly played either, and wouldn't return to the first team, but there was a buzz about up-and-coming teenage midfielder Remi Moses when he came into the side. People often talk about

Remi being the new "Degree" following Laurie's departure, especially as he sported a huge afro, but he and Laurie were very different players.

My comeback was as a substitute against Derby County in November, and my first full game of the season was a League Cup tie against Norwich. I got my first goal of the season when we drew at home with Everton – and ended up with eight that season in 26 games, which was close to my usual rate of a goal every three games.

Although the first half of the season was poor, we rallied strongly in the New Year to finish tenth in the table. But the synergy had gone and we were also struggling to overcome the disappointment of missing out on the title the previous season.

A good FA Cup run might have helped – but we lost to West Ham United in a replay, having drawn at The Hawthorns. I had some feisty battles with Alvin Martin – he was a strong lad who had forged a good partnership at the back with club stalwart Billy Bonds. But at The Hawthorns it was goalkeeper Phil Parkes who kept the Hammers in the game, making a string of cracking saves.

By now I had represented England Under-21s. Until I went to China with West Brom in the summer of 1978 I hadn't owned a British passport, so there had been some speculation about whether I could or would play for France instead, as I hailed from French Guiana. My proposed move to French club St Etienne in 1978 had hinged upon me being prepared to also play for France if selected.

Soon afterwards I was sounded out for England, and I made my debut against Denmark on 19 September 1978.

Garth Crooks scored a hat-trick but still got racist abuse from England fans, which amazed us all. Why boo your own players? After the game, we had a party in Elton John's hotel suite.

I had six run-outs for the Under-21s, and in 1982 I was an over-aged captain of the team in a match versus Denmark. My team-mates Laurie, Derek and Bryan Robson also represented England at that level – but breaking through to the senior team was a different matter. I guess we should have looked at some of our team-mates. Despite his goalscoring prowess – more than 200 goals from midfield – in the 1960s and 70s Bomber Brown had only played once for England. For many seasons he was matched by Jeff Astle, who was a legend at Albion, but he only had five full England caps to his name.

Making the breakthrough into England's senior team, managed at that time by Ron Greenwood, was going to be tough. The strong feeling around The Hawthorns was that some of our lads' efforts in both the league and UEFA Cup should have earned them senior caps. We were widely regarded as one of the best teams in the league, yet we didn't have any senior internationals.

Laurie wasn't selected until he left Albion for Real Madrid, while in Birmingham the newspapers mounted a campaign for Bryan Robson's selection for the national team. Robson was one of the finest young players of his generation and his omission seemed little short of scandalous. Getting an England call-up was very difficult for Midlands players in those days. The national press were – and still are – based mainly in London or the North-West and it was clubs in those areas which attracted most of the headlines. If you didn't play for a club in London, Manchester or Liverpool it was much harder to get into the England set-up.

You also had to play well for years to make it – although that was true for all players. Now, with so many foreign players plying their trade here, if you're English, play in the Premier League and put a good six months in, you're knocking on the door of the England squad. The game has changed.

People in football were probably more influenced by the press in those days because there were so few matches shown on TV. Albion were seen as a fading force, so we weren't in the public eye and in the papers as much as we had been the previous season. When Big Ron, Laurie and Bryan Robson had all gone, it just wasn't the same.

Robson was blossoming into a great player – and remains the best player I've played with or against. In 1980–81 he was phenomenal, which prompted a campaign orchestrated by the *Birmingham Evening Mail* to get him called up to the England team. People forget he hardly got a game for England when he was at Albion. When you consider he later clocked up 90 caps for his country, it makes you wonder how many games he would have played for England if he had broken into the full senior team earlier on.

One thing is for sure, he was always good enough. He had everything – vision, technical ability, stamina, leadership qualities, good first touch, goalscoring talent, bravery, football intelligence and strength. Most players would rate fairly well on one or two of these points. But Bryan Robson scored highly on all of them – he was top class. And yet to some, I guess, he looked wiry and, well, even a bit ordinary. He didn't seem to have an extraordinary physique, but he was a genuine box-to-box midfielder. Bryan could break a move up on the edge of our box and make up the ground to be on the end of the same move he'd started. And he wouldn't just do it once or twice in a game – he would do it repeatedly. He was undoubtedly one of the best all-round players England has ever produced.

Just like Bryan, I would have to wait for my chance. It was difficult to get into the national picture at the time as we were blessed with prolific strikers including Kevin Keegan, David Johnson, Paul Mariner, Bob Latchford, Tony Woodcock and Peter Withe. I bided my time, though, and always had a feeling I'd get that call – eventually.

On the domestic front, West Brom returned to form in the 1980–81 league season. The new guys had bedded in and we had better luck with injuries.

The happiest moment of that season for me, though, wasn't related to football – it was the birth of my son Robert on 30 October 1980. His middle name is Laurent, a nod to my early years in French Guiana. Robert was born at 7pm. I was playing a game that day, but I got a call saying that Beverley had gone into labour and I dashed off to the Queen Elizabeth Hospital in Birmingham.

Seeing your children being born is one of the landmark events of your life. You can't compare the joy of holding a child to scoring goals or anything similar, because it's a lot better. It's great to score goals, to play on the winning side in the FA Cup final and to run out in an England shirt, but seeing your child born tops it all. It was wonderful.

At the same time, I didn't understand just what I was

taking on. I was a well-known top-flight footballer cheered by thousands of adoring fans every week, but I was 22 and immature. As a father I know that I messed up a bit. I provided for my children without question, but my lifestyle outside of the home meant that I didn't give them the father they needed. I may have been a footballing role model but, looking back, I wasn't mature enough to accept the responsibility of being both a new dad and a famous player.

Football has such a laddish culture that you're not encouraged to grow up and act in a mature way. You haven't got the character. In some respects you're still finding out about yourself. Do you go home after training to change nappies or go for a few beers with the boys? For many players, it's a no-brainer.

I wasn't married when Robert was born. Beverley and I wed in 1983. *Hello!* Magazine wasn't around then to offer loads of money for exclusive pictures, but that wasn't our kind of thing anyway. A low-key ceremony at a register office witnessed by family and close friends suited us fine. We had a good first year, and I'm sure Bev thought I was going to change. Maybe I did too – I tried – but it didn't last.

Michelle was born in 1984, and once again it was amazing to see a perfect little person enter the world. By this time we had moved from our first house in Handsworth Wood to Streetly, near Sutton Coldfield. I was still juggling three elements – family, socializing and football – and probably failing miserably to get the balance right. Robert was named after my father, and Michelle was named after the Beatles song – I just loved it. Her middle name is Marie, which is also Beverley's.

Back on the field, Albion finished fourth in 1980–81. We were in with a shout of the title until the final few weeks of the campaign. The nail in our coffin was delivered in front of a packed house at Aston Villa, the eventual champions. Villa, managed by Ron Saunders, beat us 1–0, with Brendon Batson's late mistake allowing Peter Withe to nip in and score the only goal. Villa must have loved us – a few days earlier we'd hammered Ipswich, who were also challenging for the title, 4–0 at The Hawthorns.

But the real bombshell came at the end of the season. Ron Atkinson left for Manchester United, taking his assistant Mick Brown with him. Speculation had been rife for some time. But when Ron left Albion he indicated that he would come back for me, Derek Statham and Bryan Robson. It never happened. But then, it would have been difficult for Ron to buy me and Derek after he'd taken Robson and Remi Moses, as Albion were not likely to welcome more overtures from Old Trafford in the following months.

But I was even more gutted three years later when Ron took Terry Gibson from Coventry City. I was thinking, "What? Why not me?" Looking back now, I can see why. As time progressed, I wasn't playing well enough to earn a move – 1983–86 were my wilderness years.

Robson had to force his way out of West Brom, and his move became a protracted affair, which didn't help my or Derek's chances of following him out of The Hawthorns. You have to be pragmatic about these things. Managers, coaches and fellow players move on. We all have to get used to that – that's what professional football is all about – even though you hate to see your fellow players and good mates leave.

The disappointment was put aside, though, as I enjoyed my best ever season in 1981–82. I made my senior England debut, scored the goal of the season and notched up my best ever goal tally. On the downside, we lost two cup semi-finals, were nearly relegated and I got injured in the last but one game of the season, which put paid to my hopes of making the World Cup finals in Spain.

Ron's replacement, Ronnie Allen, was making a welcome return to the club. He'd worked abroad, so had lots of experience of different cultures and training methods. Because Ronnie's approach wasn't just based on hard work and lots of running, Derek Monaghan, a winger who had progressed through the ranks at Albion, went to Ronnie and said: "I don't feel fit enough – we ought to be doing more physical work." So Ronnie made him sprint and dribble the ball back to him until he was knackered and then said to him: "Do you feel fit now?"

Footballers were often conditioned to think that they had to run long distances to be physically fit, which isn't true. For me, Ronnie Allen's return was great news. In 1981–82 I was in top physical shape and really enjoying my football.

One thing Ronnie said to me was: "I don't want you coming back over the halfway line." Continental strikers didn't do that. Ronnie knew I didn't have a lot of stamina but was powerful and quick – and yet I was coming back to defend set-pieces and closing down full-backs. Ronnie wanted me to do all my work in the opposition half, where I could hurt them, and for me that was ideal because I could conserve my energy to burst past opponents. The result was my best year in football in terms of being an out-and-out goalscorer. I scored 10 goals in nine games in one spell in the middle of the season and 25 in all competitions overall.

I felt fitter and I conserved my energy better. I had very little stamina, but I'd always been like that. I always finished last in long-distance races, but when it came to the sprints I was the man to beat. Successful strikers need to have composure, and you won't have that if you are tired – you will snatch at chances and miss. If you're composed, you can set yourself before shooting and have a much better chance of scoring, which is fundamentally why you are in the side and on the pitch.

During that season, I found I was much more dynamic in terms of making runs and scoring goals. The classic one came against Norwich City in the FA Cup fifth round at The Hawthorns. It was named *Match of the Day*'s goal of the season and the trophy still has pride of place in my home. That goal was the result of being able to burst through to score. And it wasn't a one-off. When we beat Coventry City in the quarter-final I scored another explosive goal. These goals were similar to ones I scored early on in my career.

1981–82 may have been my best season on a personal level, but it was a tough one for the team. We reached two semi-finals – in the League Cup, when we lost to Spurs over two legs, and then in the FA Cup, when we went out to Second Division QPR at Highbury. Once again, for the second time in four seasons in an FA Cup semi-final, we'd failed to show up. It was a bitter pill for our fans to swallow.

Worse was to come. We drifted into a relegation battle at the end of the season. We beat Leeds United 2–0, with me scoring the all-important goal at The Hawthorns to save our skins but to send the Yorkshire club crashing down. There was little sympathy for them. Their fans didn't take the result in good grace. They rioted and tore down the railings at the Smethwick End. The press were scathing. We lost our final game to Stoke City and ended up sixth from bottom that year, which was unbelievable because the previous season we finished fourth.

Although personally I was in the form of my life, we just didn't play as a side. These were changing times for Albion. Robson and Moses had left at the start of the season, and Tony Brown was also no longer there. Andy King, Clive Whitehead, Steve Mackenzie, Martin Jol and Romeo Zondervan had joined the ranks, while Nicky Cross, Martyn Bennett, Kevin Summerfield and Monaghan had progressed from the youth team.

That season I made my England debut against Northern Ireland, coming on for the last 20 minutes. After waiting so long to get the call-up, I was determined to enjoy the moment. I took a photo of me and my son Robert, who was 18 months old, with an England flag – it's still a favourite picture of mine.

But someone with an irrational hatred of black people didn't approve of my selection. All players received fan mail and I was casually opening mine in the dressing-room when I took a closer look at the letters on one piece of paper – they'd been cut out of a newspaper and stuck down to create a chilling message – "If you put your foot on our Wembley turf you'll get one of these through your knees." Also in the envelope was a bullet wrapped in a cotton wool pad, like the ones women use to remove their make-up. That was the worst item of mail I ever received. Laurie Cunningham got far more abuse in the post than I did. We laughed about it, though – and I kept the bullet.

Racial abuse was mainly confined to the stadium. I never had individuals come up and say things to me outside the ground, on the streets or when I was out shopping. It would have been a completely different ball game if your wife and kids had been affected by the abuse and you were getting bricks thrown through your window or the car scratched. When you know it is confined to football, you can deal with it. In the early days, of course, we didn't know that. It could have escalated, so in that sense it was scary and deeply offensive.

I had played another couple of games for England that season and, with all the plaudits I was getting from the press and fellow players, I felt I was on course to make the World Cup squad. I felt good. I'd scored 25 goals, my confidence was sky-high and I was sure I would be picked. But towards the end of that game, in the process of scoring the crucial goal which ensured our survival, I pulled my hamstring.

After having treatment, I was picked for an England "A" game in Iceland. Everyone was jostling for a place, especially as England hadn't been to the World Cup finals since 1970. I was rooming with the centre-half, Steve Foster, and lost £500 to him at cards. I have never been a gambler and I haven't gambled since.

I limped off during the Iceland game and was out of the running for the tournament. I was distraught. Can you imagine how much you look forward to possibly playing in a World Cup if you've worked your way through as I had? If you have come from my kind of background – where money was always tight and you'd made so many sacrifices? I had progressed from Sunday morning and non-League football, watched by a handful of supporters – and now, just at the moment when it was all going well for me and I was in the best form of my career, I got injured right at the end of the season.

I'd even sung on England's World Cup record, "This Time We'll Get It Right" – well, I didn't. Aston Villa's Peter Withe took my place.

Although I got five England caps in total, measured in minutes my England career lasted only about one-and-a-half games. In Wales in 1982, I only got 10 minutes, and against Turkey in 1988, my final appearance in an England shirt, I only got 20. The only game I started at senior level was a friendly against West Germany, at the start of Bobby Robson's spell as manager, on 13 October 1982. The Germans won 2–1, thanks to two goals from Karl-Heinz Rumenigge. Tony Woodcock got our consolation. I played 80 minutes and thought I did OK. But I never quite made the impact I'd hoped for in an England shirt. You need to be an instant hit, but that didn't happen with me.

Closer to home, I was named Midlands player of the year and was runner-up to Kevin Keegan in the PFA player of the year awards that season.

Hindsight is a wonderful thing, I should have left West Brom in the summer of 1982 when things were going well for me. Instead, I signed another contract and that was a big mistake. Why? Because I was about to enter my wilderness years. After such a disappointing end to the 1981–82 season, what I really needed was a fresh start and a new challenge.

Nothing seemed to go right from 1982–83. I suffered several injuries and, although my goalscoring record held up, I was unsettled. The worst spell of my career was about to begin.

CHAPTER TEN
The Wilderness Years

For the best part of four seasons, I completely lost my way. Not just in football but in life. These were my wilderness years, which nearly cost me my playing career. Also, although Beverley and I had some good times during this period, it was a tricky time in our marriage.

West Brom had made a decent start to the 1982–83 season. I'd recovered from the hamstring strain which had stopped me representing England in the 1982 World Cup finals in Spain and was playing reasonably well. By January I'd scored nine goals including a hat-trick against Norwich City, and we'd continued our impressive home record against Manchester United, now managed by our old boss Ron Atkinson, by beating them 3–1. Albion weren't pulling up any trees but looked comfortable in the top half of the table.

It all started to go wrong at Upton Park, home of West Ham United, on 25 January 1983. I went for a challenge with Hammers centre-half Joe Gallagher, who was on loan from Birmingham City at the time. I flicked the ball on, and the next thing I remember was waking up in the ambulance.

I had fractured my cheekbone. I was taken to Whitechapel Hospital in East London and operated on immediately. They kept me in overnight as I needed some wire inserted to hold my cheekbone together. And I've still got it there more than 25 years on. West Brom beat the Hammers 1–0 at Upton Park, Peter Eastoe scoring our goal, but after that I only played four more league games that season.

That day set a frustrating trend. The next 18 months seemed to be a catalogue of irritating injuries. By this time Ronnie Allen had moved on once again and Ron Wylie was the manager. Every time I got injured I seemed to be coming back too early. Ron was keen to have me in the side, because I was such a key player at the club. Ron felt that my presence lifted both the players and the fans. He always wanted me back as soon as possible – and I was always keen to oblige – but that pattern began to take its toll.

I was never really 100 per cent fit, not that you can ever be in football. But you can never produce your best when you're not in tip-top shape. Also my role had changed under the new regime. Ronnie Allen hadn't wanted me crossing the halfway line to come back. Now, instead of being an out-and-out striker, I was expected to have an effect on the game in other ways. I started leading the line, coming short and showing myself more for the ball instead of running on to passes and going straight through on goal.

The main problem was that we didn't have enough creative players. If you don't have players with imagination who can lay on chances, you don't get a shot on goal. That means you have to go looking for the ball and get involved that way, when what you ought to be doing is moving away from the ball and looking to get on the end of crosses from wingers and passes from midfielders.

So in 1983–84 my footballing persona started to change from being a dynamic striker who sprinted past defenders to a more functional forward who was forced to do a variety of things just to get involved. Small wonder the goals began to dry up. And if you're not feeling in good physical shape and not scoring goals, your confidence, enjoyment and drive will begin to wane. It's a vicious circle – and getting out of it is tough.

For a host of reasons I wasn't at the top of my game. And so began a very challenging 18 months at Albion that eventually led to me leaving The Hawthorns.

Part of the problem was that I hadn't been through this kind of drop in form before. My career had always followed an upward trajectory: school, youth club, Sunday morning youth league, Athenian League, Isthmian League, First Division, Europe, England, fame and notoriety with the Three Degrees, FA Cup runs, nearly winning the championship – all fantastic achievements which had lulled me into a false sense of security. Things could only get better, surely?

Albion weren't what they had been, either. The recession under Margaret Thatcher in the early 1980s resulted in huge unemployment, notably in areas like the West Midlands, where many people worked in long-established manufacturing industries. Don't forget, the Black Country was the birthplace of the industrial revolution. Thousands of jobs were being shed, and football was a working man's game. If people weren't working they couldn't afford to watch football matches every other Saturday. Meanwhile hooliganism was reaching a peak, so the fear of trouble also kept some traditional fans away. Crowds across the country dwindled. By 1984 West Brom's gates had dipped to an average of 15,000 – almost half the size they had been five years earlier.

Under Ron Wylie the fun had gone out of training too. For my first five years at West Brom, our training sessions were mostly made up of five-a-sides. We did some sprinting and sit-ups for strength and conditioning, but mainly it was all about quick thinking and three-touch football. And the fun we were having on the training field was reflected in our attractive style of play.

Mike Kelly, Ron Wylie's assistant, was more into shape play and drills. As a coach later on in my career, I could understand what he was trying to do and could see the merit in it. But as a player I found it boring. The five-a-sides were a big part of the way we did things at Albion. They were high quality, it was hard work (boy, would we sweat) and they produced results.

Training became tortuous. I especially hated Monday mornings, when we'd have to set off on a three-mile run. I was thinking: I get whacked about holding the ball up on a Saturday, and then two days later I'm forced to go running. I hated every minute of it. One time I even got a taxi back to the training ground because I couldn't stand it. With hindsight, my attitude wasn't right.

But it wasn't just me, lots of other players were also fed up. I sat down with Ron Wylie and told him straight: "The boys aren't having it." As players you have to buy into the philosophy of the manager, otherwise it won't work. Ron had a reputation as a very good coach at Coventry, and I asked him to take the training, but he wouldn't. Mike carried on, much to our frustration. As it turned out, Ron was sacked two-thirds of the way through the 1983–84 season, with Albion languishing in the lower half of the newly-named Canon First Division (the first season the league had been sponsored). Managers were coming and going all the time – and that would continue at Albion for some time.

The personnel on the pitch had also changed. A lot of players were being shifted in and out – maybe I should have been one of them? Brendon Batson also noticed a difference: "The players coming in didn't seem to have the same attitude as some of the players in the team we had played in a few years earlier." Sadly Brendon sustained a serious knee injury which ended his career. Another great Albion player and a good friend gone. My good mate Derek Statham was out for long periods that season, while stalwart centre-backs John Wile and Ally Robertson had both left.

When the fans noticed that I was losing it, and the press began speculating that my best days had gone, it was hard to handle. I wasn't scoring many goals any more. I was top scorer with 10 goals in 1983–84, but I couldn't deal with the emotions surrounding my dip in form. And I didn't know how to dig my way out. I even started to lose my hair through stress.

I also wanted a wage rise in line with other top players. I had been an England player and I knew many of my teammates and former players at West Brom, who had moved on, were on far more money than me. Some of the figures being bandied around about how much I was asking for weren't true, but I was starting to go backwards.

When Derek Statham's son Stuart was born in January 1984, we went for a pint to wet the baby's head on the day of a match. We had an FA Cup tie that night against Rotherham, but they were Fourth Division at the time and we were expected to win easily. I had two pints of Guinness before going home for a sleep. Albion won 3–0 that night, thanks to goals from Garry Thompson and Tony Morley, and I had a good game, but that was totally unprofessional of me.

The five-a-sides would soon be back, though, under the man who'd first introduced them at Albion nine years earlier – Johnny Giles. He of course was technically the manager when I joined West Brom in 1977. It was under his regime that Ronnie Allen spotted me. But Johnny left before I started playing for the club.

In the spring of 1984 he was back at The Hawthorns. The Albion players idolized Johnny. He was the man who had turned West Brom into one of the top clubs in the country within two years of stepping through the door. He'd left for his own reasons, but was persuaded to return in March 1984, bringing Nobby Stiles and Norman Hunter with him. It would prove to be a big mistake, and although Johnny was popular when he returned, few fans protested when he left two years later.

I was initially excited by Johnny's return. I remember how highly the Albion players rated him. I wanted to absorb some of that spirit. But it didn't work out. Johnny seemed to have lost his spark – both the magic that he'd created first time around and his drive to be a top manager. He'd been managing the Republic of Ireland and Shamrock Rovers, but the First Division in England was completely different. You have to be up for it 100 per cent all the time, and I don't think Johnny's heart was quite in it any more.

It was disappointing for me, and he was probably disappointed in me, which was justified because at that point I had lost a lot of the things I'd once had. By this time I was playing up front alongside Garry Thompson, who was excellent to work with. He was a powerful header of the ball, but with me not playing well, hamstrung by injuries and always coming back too soon, the combination never felt right. I still had to learn when to play with a certain amount of pain and when it is best not to play with pain.

One of Johnny's major decisions during his second spell in charge was to sell me in October 1984 – and I hardly objected. I wasn't enjoying my football but fancied an upward move to one of the country's bigger clubs. The trouble was, the general impression of me was that I'd gone. I was no longer the force I used to be.

Johnny wanted to change things around. He wanted some money to make that happen. I was already a high wage earner but still wanted an increase, even though I wasn't playing well. I didn't know how to turn it around, because I had never been in a trough before, so he sold me to Coventry City.

Johnny and I have spoken about this recently. He felt I had got complacent and was not producing the goods. He also wanted a big man/small man combination up front, so I didn't fit the bill. Later he brought in Garth Crooks and Imre Varadi. For a time he was successful – but in the long run it didn't work out.

Bobby Gould was Coventry's manager at the time. Later he became a much maligned character within football with an up-and-down managerial career, but Bobby nonetheless signed many good players at value for money prices. He tabled a £250,000 bid for me. I doubt Bobby himself expected Albion to accept his offer. A few months earlier chairman Bert Millichip had gone on record saying he doubted Albion would get much more than £600,000 – so it was doubtful I would leave. Now it seemed that £250,000 would do.

I have never been a good gambler and I got this one spectacularly wrong. I had wanted to move to a big club, but to be honest, I was happy to leave Albion – but I really didn't want to go to Coventry. I'd gone along with it, however, thinking that as soon as it got into the papers that Coventry were looking to sign me, better clubs would come in. But no one did.

That's how low my game had sunk. £250,000 was a small sum to pay for someone with my track record. I was only 26. Just two years earlier I was ready to go to the World Cup with England and was second behind Kevin Keegan in the PFA player of the year awards. Decent players were routinely being transferred for £1 million. Surely someone in the middle ranks of the First Division would have fancied taking a punt on me for that price? The market, though, reflects your standing within the game.

Derek Statham tried to persuade me to stay, but I was hurt and shocked. "Right," I said, "I'm going to go to Coventry to show them how good I am." Derek told me recently: "I didn't want you to go, but maybe that was just me being selfish. Around the time your form dipped in 1983–84, the club had been through a lot of turmoil. I don't feel West Brom put up much of a fight to keep you."

Coventry hadn't been out of the bottom six for many seasons before I arrived at Highfield Road, so it was a massive step down for me. Also, within two months Bobby Gould had gone. A 5–2 hammering on my return to Albion at the end of November didn't help. I wasn't emotionally committed to Coventry for another two years. And so my poor form carried on. The turning point would only come much later, with John Sillett's appointment as manager in 1986.

I was a big fish in a small pond at Coventry. Everything was targeted on me. It was a horrible time. I'd had two years left on my contract at WBA. What I should have done was dig in, wait for my form to return at Albion, and then move. Form is temporary, talent is permanent.

Bobby Gould's sacking meant the manager who signed me and believed in me had gone. I remember thinking: "What the hell have I done?" I felt I'd made a really bad decision. Don Mackay and Frank Upton came in. Don was a nice chap, but we didn't like the training under Frank.

At the end of each of the first couple of seasons we had to endure last-day battles to stay up. Things got so bad that on a Friday afternoon Micky Gynn, Dave Bennett and I used to go to a pub in Coventry city centre called The Bug and Black Bat to have a couple of pints of Guinness. That would have been well out of order at West Brom – but that was the mood at Coventry. So what? We didn't care. And we weren't enjoying it. It was a really low period.

For me, a big part of it was that I knew I'd made a wrong decision. I kept thinking: I shouldn't be here. Coventry's fans probably felt the same. But they'd got used to that sort of disappointment. My failure to impress, despite having a big name and good reputation, wasn't an unfamiliar story for the Sky Blues. They'd seen it all before. They'd had their hopes dashed so many times and had few expectations other than survival.

If going to Coventry was a bad choice, it nearly got worse. Wolves were tumbling through the leagues and were in Division Three at the time (the following season they'd be in Division Four). In 1985 Coventry tried to sell me to Wolves for £40,000. As if my confidence wasn't low enough.

I confronted the management about this and they denied it. But it was clear that Coventry were desperate to recoup anything they could for me. I was on the slide, they were on the slide, so they tried to get rid of me. I was so frustrated. Every day was a struggle. I was low on confidence and in a deep, deep hole which I couldn't seem to dig myself out of. That's how far things had descended. In 1982 I was ranked one of the top players in the country. Three years later, a club which didn't want me was trying to sell me for £40,000.

It all started with that incident at West Ham. Because of the insistence on getting me back into the team at West Brom as quickly as possible, mostly without playing any reserve-team games, I'd never recovered physically or mentally. It soon began to have an effect on my form, and now it was all starting to go wrong. I only scored five goals in each of the first two seasons I was at Coventry. Ten goals in 65 appearances. Things had to change.

Thank goodness for John Sillett and George Curtis. John had been youth team coach and George had been the club's commercial director. In April 1986 they took charge after Don Mackay had been dismissed with Coventry lying 19th in the table and with just three games of the season remaining. They split the roles. John was the coach, while George took on the mantle of director of football/general manager. They knew each other from their playing days at the club, so they had developed a strong partnership.

At the end of the 1985–86 season John told us that if we won two out of our last three games of the season to stay up they would take us to Magaluf on the island of Majorca for a week's holiday. So we beat Stoke, Luton and Everton to book our flights. We'd never won three games on the trot before, but did so to ensure our survival. The season before, we'd had to beat QPR on the final day of the season to stay up. In a perverse way it showed we had character. It was dreadful that we had been there in the first place – but at least we had the bottle to win crucial games.

So they took us to Magaluf. We drank in the London Bar every day and had a fantastic time. That set the tone for things to come. I have never drunk so much in my life as I did during the following season. That is how John and George engendered team spirit. We trained together, played together and socialized together. It was great.

In Magaluf, John craftily went around the players asking each of us, quite casually, how we wanted to play. And he took notice. Ask most footballers and they'll tell you they want to play to feet. We want to play passing football. Most players want to get on the ball and express themselves. Very few will say knock it long and we'll chase it – least of all me with my small lungs.

Through watching on the training ground before he even took over, John had soon realized I wasn't being brought into the team in the right way. He recognized my key physical attributes – my upper body and leg strength, balance and chest control – and he knew that when Ron Atkinson was in charge at West Brom I was used to having the ball played to my feet. I might have been the best-known player in the Coventry side, but it wasn't just about me – I was desperate to be part of a successful team again. John told me recently: "You could have scored 30 goals a season but were unselfish – you always wanted to set up chances for your team-mates."

So they used that week away to find out about us as individuals. Then when we returned to Coventry they changed things around. Lots of five-a-sides, lots of fun. If we didn't have a midweek game we'd work really hard on the training ground on Tuesday. Overall they built up a great team spirit and instilled confidence in the players. All the ingredients you need to win things. It was the best team spirit I experienced anywhere – at any of the clubs I played for – and 1986–87 turned out to be the most productive season in my career.

A large part of it was built on drinking and socializing, and they used the drinking culture in football to their advantage. Coventry had an acclaimed restaurant at the ground, and once a month they laid on a five-course meal with champagne, the works. Before every FA Cup game they would take us away, either to Bournemouth or to Fuengirola on the Costa del Sol in Spain, where we'd live it up, socialize and drink.

We were encouraged to go out and enjoy ourselves, but were urged to book a taxi on the club. They didn't want you drinking and driving – but you could go out and get smashed. The golden rule was: don't drink pints, always have halves. If they caught you with a pint glass you'd be fined. So you could be hit with a £5 fine for having a pint of orange juice or milk, but guzzling dozens of halves of beer was no problem. You're thinking there's a slight inconsistency there, but the aim was not to appear like lager louts by swigging out of pint glasses.

Let me tell you about my team-mates. The skipper was Brian Kilcline, a fearsome-looking centre-half and a key presence in the dressing-room. Killer would do the most incredible things. I remember him thinking he'd put on a bit too much timber over the summer, so he started his pre-season training wearing about four shirts, a bin-liner and three layers of tracksuit bottoms. He looked like the Michelin Man with all this clobber on. He must have lost about 12 pounds in the training session, and he was so dehydrated and drained – unhealthily so – that we all thought he would pass out. That was the sort of far-out character Killer was. He was very funny and used to make us all laugh.

Killer's partner in the heart of the defence was Trevor Peake. He was magnificent and rarely put a foot wrong – he was our Mr Consistency and in my view one of the most underrated players of his day. He should have won loads of England caps. Why not? In my opinion, it's because he played for an unfashionable Midlands club. I'd seen it all before at West Brom. Great players like Tony Brown, Laurie Cunningham and Bryan Robson, all overlooked despite being the best in their positions in the country.

Trevor suffered from that. He was phenomenal. I'd played with the likes of John Wile, Ally Robertson and Paul McGrath, who were all top defenders and extremely reliable players, but I would rate Trevor's ability to read the game as among the best. At the back, Killer would go around bashing people, while Trevor was the calming influence who would read the game carefully and position himself to react and make the right tackle or intercept a cross or pass. He also played the ball out well.

Brian Borrows was another underrated player – a really good defender. He had a great partnership down the right with Dave Bennett, who could run with the ball and had bags of skill.

Up front there were frequent changes – Coventry kept buying strikers – but it was always me and somebody else. I played up front with Keith Houchen for two seasons. He couldn't score in the league to save his life but in the cup he was like Roy of the Rovers. He had a fantastic cup run in 1987. The best strike partner I had at Coventry was Dave Bennett, who was mainly a winger but as a strike partner he played off me very well.

Gary Bannister was OK when he was there, and I did well with Kevin Gallacher, who was a good forward. Alan Brazil and Kevin Drinkell were also there briefly. It didn't quite work with David Speedie, although he was fantastic coming on to the ball rather than holding the ball up.

Our goalie Steve Ogrizovic was Mr Coventry. He was also a good cricketer who played for Coventry and North Warwickshire in the Birmingham League – in fact, cricket was his first love. Oggy was super-fit and had a great attitude. He was a policeman before joining Shrewsbury Town and then moving on to Coventry – another astute Bobby Gould signing.

Like most keepers Oggy was a bit odd. If he didn't have his pre-match meal at a quarter to twelve he'd be moaning. Goalkeepers are strange people. If a goalkeeper is normal you have to question him. They're all a bit suspect. But if they've got an edge to them they'll probably make it as a goalie. Oggy hated it if you chipped him in training. He'd chase after you shouting, "You wouldn't do that in a game!" He also fancied himself as an outfield player – but he was rubbish, as most goalies are. He used to do this turn, which we called the Oggy Turn, and he'd always end up standing on somebody's toe.

The fittest lad was David Phillips. He had incredible energy levels. Nicky Pickering would run up and down the left-hand side all day. Greg Downs was a solid defender who had been Norwich's left-back for 10 years. Micky Gynn was a great little player coming forward from midfield. He also had an impressive soul and jazz collection and still collects rare records.

Lloyd McGrath was a great man-marker. We used to call him Man Friday. He would get battered and bruised and spend most of the week on the treatment table. He had the highest pain threshold of anyone I played with. He would dive into 60–40 tackles against opponents which weren't in his favour all the time on the edge of the box and we'd think, "Lloydy, why? You don't need to do that!" John Sillett used to say to him: "Lloydy, get the ball and give it to someone who can play." Lloyd wouldn't say boo to a goose off the pitch until he was drunk – then you couldn't shut him up He'd be a funny guy then.

The dynamics of that atmosphere were engineered by George and John. It might seem quite unsophisticated, now that we know so much more about fitness, physiology, diet and nutrition, but it worked. George was tough. He never wore tracksuit bottoms in training – he always wore shorts and always played in goal because he had a dodgy knee from an injury harking back to his playing days. When we smashed the ball into him he would not flinch.

John was a true football man. He brought humour, direction, confidence, swagger and belief. He believed we were better than we were and he encouraged us to think that too.

Even if I say so myself I played well. But it was fun because we were encouraged to express ourselves. To get my confidence back and to enjoy playing and going to training again was a wonderful feeling. I regained the passion for the game I'd had throughout my early days at West Brom. When you are getting caned in the press, you have to have belief in yourself, and that came flooding back. I believed in myself, and it was the same for the other players.

Even though we were drinking a lot, we worked hard. And if we didn't play well, we still drank to cheer ourselves up. On Tuesdays after the training-ground blow-out we'd go to The Blacksmiths in Ryton-on-Dunsmore. That was to Coventry what The Marksman had been to West Brom. It's where you'd find us after training and for most of the rest of the day. The laughter, banter and larking about was a real tonic after those dark days towards the end of my spell at The Hawthorns.

John was a shrewd man, though. Not long after he took over he pulled me aside and said: "Cyrille, I'm going to have a good go at you every now and then and I don't want you to react. I'm going to have a right pop at you, but don't respond angrily." What he wanted to do was use me as an example of a player he could shout at to get his message across. He knew what the other lads would think. Well, he's had a go at Cyrille, and he didn't react, so I won't. Smart psychology. I was an England player and the biggest name there – so if I had reacted and showed disrespect, the rest would have been unsettled. That isn't what John wanted.

If he said, "Regis – you're this, you're that and the other," I'd stand there and take it. Then he'd turn to someone else and say. "And as for you ..." They'd think, fair enough, Cyrille's taken a blast, so I'd better not react angrily either. John didn't do it all the time – he was selective – but it worked. We would get a right rollocking but react positively.

In our circle a rollocking was called "digging someone out". It meant you were being singled out for having not pulled your weight, and when that happened John could really lay into you. Players don't like being "dug out", but they do like winning and walking out at Wembley before an FA Cup final – and that's what would happen to us next.

CHAPTER ELEVEN
All Sing Together

I have never drank as much in my life as I did during our triumphant FA Cup-winning season of 1986–87 – but then I never had so much confidence either.

We were a tight unit at Coventry. We liked each other for a start, and deep down most of us knew we were better players now than at any stage of our careers. Bobby Gould had brought many of us to the club, including Trevor Peake, Steve Ogrizovic, Micky Gynn, Dave Bennett and me. We were the core of the side.

Throughout that season, we had amazing levels of confidence. We'd had to fight to stay in Division One for three seasons on the trot, and now suddenly we realized things were starting to gel. John Sillett and George Curtis noticed it too, and they carried us forward. It would be an amazing season.

We developed an ability to run for each other, and a lot of this came from being great mates and socializing together. Players could tell each other off and – because of the social dynamics – it wasn't taken amiss. Afterwards we'd have a laugh about it. If someone said, "Sort yourself out," you'd react and everyone took it the right way. You didn't go thinking, "The so-and-so – I'll get him back." You'd think,

148

"Fair enough – he's got a point ... but I'll remind him what he called me later over a drink."

Training was great fun, and when that was over we were encouraged to socialize. It was all about building team spirit, and the management realized that was just as important as discipline and tactics.

Most of the time we found cheap and cheerful ways to have fun. Whenever we were playing away, as soon as we got to the hotel, a few of us used to get all the ice together from our minibar fridges, put it in the sink in someone's room and put some beers in there, so they were nice and chilled. We'd sit down for a meal at 7pm, then go back to the room, have a chat, have a beer and play cards before going to bed. Then we'd play well the following day. John and George didn't know too much about it, but they didn't ask. They were old school, and as long as you acted sensibly and did things on the quiet they were OK.

I know what some of you may be thinking. This "all lads together" and bonding stuff is taking the players away from their families – and that isn't conducive to stable relationships. That isn't how it was. My foibles with seeing other women outside my marriage were my fault and no one else's.

There wasn't a Mother's Day or wife's birthday that went by without the club sending them a lovely bouquet of flowers. Every few months the girls would have their own night out in Coventry – they would go to a good restaurant, all expenses paid by the club.

It wasn't all play – it had a purpose. Tuesdays were always a blast – lots of running – and we all accepted it. It was the other side of all the drinking and socializing, and that was fair enough.

Under John Sillett, we'd do a continuous run around the pitch, then do one side fast, the rest slow, then two sides fast, two sides slow, etc.

I remember we had a letter from a fan who wrote to us saying: "You lot aren't fit – I do lots of cross country running and I could out-run you lot. You're rubbish." So John invited him in – on a Tuesday. And this bloke brought his girlfriend with him. She was presumably going to be impressed by him outstripping us and showing us how fit he was. Anyway he couldn't keep up with us and he ended up being sick – right in front of his girlfriend. He didn't write to us again. He might have been a strong long-distance runner, but football training is different. Whatever is said about footballers and the supposed lack of effort they put in, most of them are seriously fit.

One of the other things that set John apart from most managers was that he never had a post-match debrief straight after the game – he'd always leave it until the Monday. He would study the video over the weekend then choose his words carefully, having double-checked what he had seen, so his comments were considered rather than hasty.

The players respected him for that. We were coming out of darkness into light. What had been a long, boring 40-minute drive to training suddenly seemed to take five minutes. I wanted to be there – to hop out of the car and be with my mates. I no longer just wanted to go training then go home as soon as possible.

The tactics at Coventry were all about me holding the ball up. We played entertaining football, passing and moving and hitting me with the ball. Micky Gynn would come off me,

Lloyd McGrath would sit in midfield, while Dave Bennett went wide right and Nick Pickering played wide left. It was an attacking side. John was very much like Big Ron. He knew how to build a side and motivate everyone.

Throughout that season we were only mid-table, but for Coventry that was incredible. There was a sense of belonging in the top flight – and we felt it was our turn to win the FA Cup.

The first match in our run was at home in the third round. We had a 3–0 victory over Bolton Wanderers, who were then in the Third Division. I remember rounding the goalkeeper and scoring. Then Keith Houchen started his amazing run of cup goalscoring. That was our only game at Highfield Road in the cup that year – all our other games would be away, so we reached Wembley the hard way.

In the fourth round we really upped our game, beating Manchester United 1–0 at Old Trafford. It was Alex Ferguson's first season in charge at United, and we played in front of 49,000 people on a pitch half covered in frost. Houchen scored a scrappy goal, bundling the ball over the line from David Phillips's flick-on. We had to soak up some pressure and it was a great win. After this result our confidence levels soared, and I remember listening intently to the draw for the next round with the other lads in the dressing-room. When we drew Stoke away, who were in the Second Division at the time, we really began to sense that we could progress even further.

Despite the crowds dropping off in the 1980s, the FA Cup was still a big competition for fans and for clubs – not like today when it only seems to get serious for Premier League sides in the final few rounds. Back then, lots of clubs really fancied their chances of winning the FA Cup, and there was always tension when cup weekend came around. Everybody spoke about the FA Cup as the glamour trophy.

The Stoke game was a noisy, hard-fought Midlands derby, and we were determined to win. We've beaten Man United, we were thinking – we can't lose to Stoke. The same way that at West Brom we used to believe we could win every game, that's how we felt at Coventry in 1987.

But Stoke were a really tough nut to crack on a heavy pitch. Micky Gynn got the winning goal, but they had a couple of half chances and Oggy was forced to make some timely saves to keep Stoke at bay. He was fantastic that season. I won the Midlands player of the year award, but Oggy was Coventry City's player of the year. He would repeat his heroics in the semi-final against Leeds and was on top of his game.

In the quarter-final we drew Sheffield Wednesday at Hillsborough. We were underdogs going there, but were cheered on by 15,000 hopeful Sky Blues fans. I put us in front with a goal that indicated I was back to my old ways. Lloyd McGrath slipped the ball to me on the centre circle, I laid it off first time to Bennett, spun away, and then he repaid the compliment. I took a couple of touches and hit the ball early from the edge of the box into the net. It was a quality moment. That's what happens when you're oozing confidence as a striker, and that was what I had been missing.

As a striker if you hit the target you have a chance. Sometimes you curl a shot, but if you aim for the biggest part of the goal you have the best opportunity. You can aim for the corner, but if you drag it wide you can't score. Hit it true and hit the target – it's as simple as that. It's all about percentages. If you are coming from wide hit it across the keeper – if he spills it, there's a good chance someone else will follow it in. If you shoot near the post, it looks great when it goes in but a disaster when it goes wide.

That goal set the tone of the rest of the game. When they're at home, teams have to come at you. We liked to attack too, so it was perfect for us because we could counter-attack. Wednesday had to come at us. Gary Megson equalized for them in the second half, but then Houchen put us 2–1 ahead with a deflected goal, and his second goal made it 3–1 to put the result beyond doubt.

Winning away from home galvanizes you. Again that meant a few more late nights and some more beers – the usual stuff for us.

Ironically we returned to Hillsborough to meet Leeds in the semi-final. In 1987 Leeds were a Second Division club but they were going well at the time. The bookies even made them slight favourites.

It was a good day weather-wise. I remember driving to Coventry to get the coach. I had a BMW at the time and I picked up a couple of the boys, Benno and Gynny, on the way. We were playing a bit of reggae music. Gynny was the club's music man – he loved R 'n' B, soul, reggae and jazz, chilled-out stuff. He would pay £200 for an album, and he had rows and rows and rows of them at home. One day Gynny even went out training with a hood up, his earphones on and a Walkman in his pocket. He was one of the boys – he laughed a lot and was good at cards – and today he'll still buy rare grooves. Only now he has to fork out £600 for some of them.

The sun was shining, I was driving, my team-mates were chilling and we were having a fantastic time. In the hotel there was a positive atmosphere and, if we were nervous, we didn't show it.

The semi-final was bittersweet for me, though, as I should have scored a hat-trick. Leeds took the lead, scoring from a corner, and the goal was all my fault. David Rennie – the man I was supposed to be marking – had scored.

Oggy pulled off a good save to prevent Leeds going two up, and I had a couple of chances. I received the ball with my back to goal. I flicked it round the defender and spanked it from an angle but it hit the side netting.

Then another chance came – an easier one. I got my head on to a cross but couldn't make it count. I think, looking back, because I made that mistake which led to the Leeds goal, I wasn't relaxed enough. I was edgy. I wanted to make up for my mistake and was anxious. But I needed to control my emotions and the tension. Come on, Cyrille, you've already played in three semi-finals with West Brom.

At half-time I trudged into the dressing-room and put my hands up. "Sorry lads," I said, "the goal was my fault and I should have scored a couple too." John Sillett was doing his team talk and we were quiet. He then gave some of us a tot of whisky to relieve the tension. We were down for the first time in months. We had such great team spirit, and now the edge had been taken off things.

Then suddenly in the corner there was this sound. It began very quietly: "Here we go, here we go, here we go." It was Lloyd McGrath. Of all people – Lloyd, our Man Friday, usually the quietest lad in the dressing-room. Gradually we all started to pick up on it. "Here we go, here we go, here we go." Gynny, myself, Peaky: "Here we go, here we go, here we go." And it got louder and louder and louder until everyone had linked arms around each other's shoulders and it rose in a crescendo.

In the end, everyone in the whole room – the kit man, the players, the backroom staff, John and George – was singing at the top of their voices. It went on for what seemed ages, and then we said: "C'mon, let's get out there and let's win this game."

What an incredible lift that was. What a fantastic sporting moment and a real display of unity. It touched us in a way I don't think any of us could really explain. It was born out of the difficulties of fighting to stay up on the last day of the season, the years of "Regis – where have you been, you're crap." Some of these boys had been in the backwaters, like Gynny at Peterborough and Dave Bennett at Man City and Cardiff. They were used to survival battles; now they were fighting for a place in the FA Cup final.

It just exploded – it was an outpouring of emotion. This was where all that bonding, all that drinking, socializing, laughing and joking came to fruition. We were brothers. These guys were my best mates and we desperately wanted to get to Wembley. Leeds must have heard it. Along with the referee and linesmen, ground staff and FA officials. Now our challenge was to transmit that emotion into our performance. Leeds didn't stand a chance. They didn't know what was about to hit them.

The first key moment was Gynny's equalizer. Benno set it up. Leeds defender Brendan Ormsby hesitated. Benno slid in, hooked the back in and crossed from the right touchline. Lloyd McGrath had a swipe and missed it, but luckily Gynny raced into the box and scored.

I dived in on Gynny, hugged him and shouted, "I love you, man. I love you." Because I was off the hook. I wouldn't let the poor fella go. It was great for the team – but he'd also saved my bacon.

Keith Houchen – who else? – made it 2–1 after rounding the keeper and scoring from a narrow angle. Then, with minutes to go, Leeds brought on a sub, striker Keith Edwards. Gynny went for a tackle on the edge of the box – with his wrong foot – and got rolled. The cross came in and Edwards scored straight away with a header to make it 2–2. We were gutted.

The momentum was now with Leeds. The rousing "Here we go" chant was now a distant memory. Extra time was understandably edgy. It was nip and tuck and nothing particularly happened at first as everyone was getting tired. I was knackered. Cyrille Regis – a Rolls-Royce with a Mini engine. It was all about mental strength now. Physically I was finished – and I wasn't the only one.

We won a free-kick on the edge of the box. I had cramp by now, but I still managed to get up and nod the ball back into space. Man of the moment Keith Houchen got a touch then Benno toe-poked it home. Oh, the relief!

Now they had to come at us. Oggy made two fantastic saves and we saw the game out. The final whistle when you've won an FA Cup semi-final must be one of the sweetest sounds ever.

The Coventry fans went absolutely wild. We went over to them to celebrate. I had mixed feelings, because deep down

I knew I could have had a hat-trick, but we were through. Yes, bittersweet.

As a striker you tend to remember when you miss a chance or open goal because that is what you are there to do – score goals. It did affect me – in the same way that when I scored great goals I experienced such elation.

I always did my best to stay on an even keel – you try to avoid getting too high on the highs or too low on the lows. But it is inevitable as a striker because you live and play on the edge – it can be a fine line between winning and losing. The goalscorers in the team, although they rely on other players to create the chances, are usually the ones who stick the ball in the back of the net – and when you do that the fans adore you and remember you.

Reaching the FA Cup final meant everything to us. To the fans it was brilliant. The club had reached a major final for the first time in its 104-year history. For me, it was finally a chance to win something in football. Not many people get to win anything in the game. It was also a chance to erase the memory of losing two previous FA Cup semi-finals when I was at West Brom.

The party started on the way back from Hillsborough, with fans celebrating on the coaches and in cars. People dressed their dogs in sky-blue gear, and the city was on a high for the entire month leading up to the May final. You don't realize what football means to a community until something like that happens.

I grew up within a stone's throw of Wembley Stadium. When I was 15 or 16 they built a hotel nearby and I applied for a waiter's job there, but I didn't even get that. I used to go past

Wembley on the No. 18 bus when I was travelling to Harrow College to study as an apprentice electrician. We used to go to Alperton Boys' Club to play table tennis and five-a-side football. The legendary stadium was part of the landscape of my youth. But I didn't really appreciate, while I was growing up, just how important it was to the fans of a football club to reach a major final at Wembley.

There was something else. In the 1980s, Coventry had been ravaged by industrial decline and unemployment. It made life in the city and the wider West Midlands miserable for many people. Generations of the same families had worked in the car industry, and when factories shut down it was a hammer blow to these communities.

Coventry City Football Club was a shining beacon at the time. I didn't realize what it meant until I experienced and was part of it. As a player you know the game is all about the fans – but this was tangible.

We visited the Peugeot factory and the boys working there shouted at us, "Come on!" The whole thing gave us such a buzz. This is what you go into football for – to put a smile on people's faces and to be part of something that is special and rare. It is usually all too brief – but most players don't get to experience it at all.

Personally, I was undergoing a renaissance and loving it. I was getting back to the good run of form that I'd enjoyed early in my career and it felt great. At the time of the final I was 29 and had been a professional footballer for 10 years. Although I'd seemingly been through a lot and had survived a horrible, tough period, I was now back in the limelight and loving every minute.

During the build-up to the final, I met the sprinter John Regis for the first time. We met when being photographed together as part of the Cup Final publicity. I guess it made a good story to bring together two notable black sportsmen with the same family name from the same island. Apparently we're distant cousins somewhere down the line. John's family, like mine, are from St Lucia and we must join up somewhere. Just as I grew up in West London, John was raised in South London after all his dad's family, including his brothers, migrated to England. As it happens, both John and I now work for the same great sports agency, the Stellar Group, run by Jonathan Barnett and David Mannaseh.

The Coventry lads also went on the children's TV programme *Blue Peter* wearing our smart sky-blue tracksuits. Everything that any of us earned from any media work was put into a pool. Benno and I even had our photographs taken wearing two-tone suits in honour of Coventry bands The Specials and The Selecter, who kick-started the Ska revival in 1979.

It was all good fun. We recorded the obligatory Cup Final tune in someone's front room in Keresley. There were cans of lager everywhere. It was low budget, and we couldn't sing, but we had a good laugh.

It didn't catch on. As the sun shone all the Coventry fans wanted to sing was their anthem "All Sing Together", famously adapted in 1962 by manager Jimmy Hill and director John Camkin to the tune of the Eton Boating Song. The original song starts: "Jolly boating weather ..." – and certainly those were the climatic conditions on 16 May 1987 for the staging of the 106th FA Cup Final.

To prepare we went to Bournemouth for three days as usual. We had a couple of press meetings, but other than that it was the normal routine. As well as a few drinks, our fun-packed programme included games of golf, in which the serious golfers would play up front and the hackers – me, Peaky, Lloyd McGrath and Killer – would go round at the back. We also ran dodgy shirt competitions – we used to go to Oxfam to find the loudest shirts we could find.

We did some training and tactical work, but otherwise we went out and enjoyed ourselves. It may have been Cup Final week – but we weren't going to change the routine which had served us so well.

John Sillett had a friend who ran a pub called The Lamb in the New Forest. We would get there on a Sunday for 1pm and he would close the pub for us. We would have some drinks there before heading on to Bournemouth for a night out.

After three days in Bournemouth we headed back to Coventry on the Wednesday. It was then off again to Marlow, on the Thames, to stay at the Compleat Angler Hotel on the night before the final.

Most people outside Coventry believed it was Tottenham's cup, because their team was chock-full of internationals like Ray Clemence, Chris Hughton, Mitchell Thomas, Gary Mabbutt, Richard Gough, Steve Hodge, Ossie Ardiles, Paul Allen, Clive Allen, Glenn Hoddle and Chris Waddle. They were all internationals – whereas we had just one, Welshman David Phillips. The remainder of our team was English. I had played at Wembley for England before, but Dave Bennett was the only one who'd experienced a final there.

However, we felt we had the edge on them, and we knew we had the character to beat them. We also had confidence, because we had beaten Tottenham 4–3 at Christmas, when I scored the winning goal with seconds to go.

The night before the final we wanted to stick to our usual routine, so we asked if we could have a few beers. John Sillett said OK, but not at the hotel. So we went into town and bought some beer from the off licence, went back to the hotel and chilled.

There was a wedding party at the hotel on the day of the final and they were going to the church across the River Thames in a boat, so we had some photos taken with them. Killer, being Killer, took the garter of the girl getting married. It got passed down the bus with the lads smelling her expensive perfume.

We left the hotel in our sponsored suits. Seeing the fans around Wembley lifted our spirits straight away, and walking around the pitch before the game was a special experience.

I felt a mixture of excitement and apprehension, and I recall a slight fear of failure. No matter how confident we were that we would win – that we, maybe, had one over on Spurs – there was still this lingering doubt that only one of us had been there before and he'd been on the losing side. How would we perform? Tottenham had players who could have torn us apart if they hit their peak and we didn't. They were a top-drawer side and were being paid a lot more money than we were. We later found out that they picked up £14,000 each for losing, while we got £2,500 each for winning.

It was a classic underdogs versus favourites confrontation. They were well-honed thoroughbreds. Ossie Ardiles was a

World Cup winner, while Glenn Hoddle was one of the finest British players of his generation. We were mainly misfits who had been recruited from all sorts of clubs, usually at a time when things weren't going well for us.

John Sillett didn't care about that, though. He led us out rather than George and I can still see his face now. He was so proud, and the way he went about things touched the ordinary man in the street. They understood John because he spoke their language. He was likeable, very funny, and showed his emotions – the press loved him. He and George also had Coventry in their blood and still love the club today.

It was a lovely sunny day. And the pitch was soft – maybe a little too soft, as we found out during extra time. We walked up the slight incline on to the pitch and blinked into the sunlight. It was a metaphor for my career at that point. In the dim and distant days of the wilderness years, all I could envisage was a bleak future and a once glittering career waning before my eyes. Now I was a member of a rejuvenated group of players who would die for each other, who played with steely determination and with smiles on their faces. A group who, on their day, would match one of England's finest teams to lift Coventry's only major trophy – the FA Cup.

Led by our proud peacock, our manager John Sillett, we'd earned our day in the sun. It was the highlight of my career, and my family, including Beverley and my brother David, were there to share it with me.

As the light hits you, so does this wall of rapturous cheers. Walking out to the centre circle, I looked around for the people I knew and thought: "How did I get here and what will happen?"

Left: Wearing Three Lions on my chest, this is for England B in a 1–1 draw with Iceland in 1982.

Right: My second England cap was as a substitute against Wales in April 1982.

Left: The West Brom photocall in August 1983, my last full season with the Baggies.

Above: I use my pace to get between Spurs' Ossie Ardiles (left) and Chris Hughton during the FA Cup Final.

Right: It was great to be part of Coventry's first ever FA Cup victory in 1987. I am celebrating with the team (far left, back).

Above: There's no better feeling in football than carrying off a cup, and the biggest in English club football is the FA Cup. In 1987, with Coventry City, it was my time.

Above: I joined Aston Villa in 1991 and scored 11 goals in my first season at Villa Park.

Right: Getting the better of Gary Mabbutt for Villa against Spurs at Villa Park in the FA Cup third round in 1992. We drew 0–0, and won the replay at White Hart Lane 1–0, but were knocked out by Liverpool in the quarter-finals.

Right: My move to Wolves in 1993–94 saw me drop out of the top division for the first time in 16 years.

Below: Two veterans in action: 36-year-old John Wark of Ipswich does the splits over me, aged 35.

Above: After retiring as a player I wanted to stay in football and used my coaching qualification to train the reserves at West Brom.

Left: Coaching on the touchline during West Brom's League Cup tie against Liverpool at the Hawthorns in 1997. I soon realised that coaching was not for me and resigned.

Above: HM The Queen pins the medal making me a Member of the Order of the British Empire on my chest. I was so proud.

Below: Cyrille Regis, MBE. With me at Buckingham Palace is my wife Julia.

Above: My beautiful daughter Michelle with me.

Left: Three generations, left to right, my son Rob, his son Riley and me.

Right: Me, the grandfather, with Michelle's daughters Jayda (left) and Renée, in 2009.

The eyes of the world are upon you. You feel the weight of the FA Cup's history, tradition and mysticism. I saw our fans in blue and white, frantically waving banners. As I shook the Duchess of Kent's hand, I tried to focus, telling myself: don't forget to do the thing you've worked on, don't lose the player you're marking at set-pieces; don't tense up if a chance comes along. Stay calm and enjoy it. If we win, boy, what a night this will be!

We made a disastrous start. Many of us hadn't even touched the ball and it was in the back of the net courtesy of Clive Allen at the near post. A goal down within three minutes – I began to fear the worst, like a 4–0 thumping. That's when the insecurities start to come out and you begin to question yourself. Are you good enough? Did you really think for one moment that you could win the FA Cup?

I remember saying to Keith Houchen, as we got the ball to restart the match, let's keep this down to two or three – but in a jokey way. That early goal opened up the game. We have to get back in it. We have to react, otherwise we'll lose, we'll die, we'll fail. It's not what we came here for.

It was time to roll up our sleeves and get that equalizer. With nine minutes gone, I went wide and slipped the ball to Greg Downs. He crossed, Houchen got the flick-on and Bennett nipped in between Ray Clemence and the defender and hit it, off balance, into the net – with his left foot.

Benno scored with his left foot? It's purely for standing on. And at Wembley. Man, oh man, this really isn't supposed to happen.

For the remainder of the half we were pressing hard, but it was Spurs who went closest. Peaky and Oggy got in a muddle and Clive Allen nipped in, only to hit the side netting. At the other end, Gynny was played in and he was one on one with Clemence, but the experienced keeper came out on top.

Five minutes before half time, Hoddle teed up a free-kick. There was confusion in our back line and Gary Mabbutt popped up to score. Killer had lost him and Oggy was off his line.

At half-time, we were all feeling down as we walked back to the dressing-room. There were no chants of "Here we go" this time. John Sillett urged us to keep pushing and after 64 minutes we scored the equalizer everyone always remembers. It's Houchen again. Oggy punted it up field and I flicked it on to Keith, who in turn played it out to Benno. Our nippy right-winger jinked one way, then the other, and sent in a cracking cross which Houchen launched himself at to make it 2–2. As diving headers go, that was top drawer.

Houchen dived over the hoardings towards our fans to celebrate, but no one followed him. We had to conserve energy on the strength-sapping Wembley turf. Spurs created more chances and Killer got injured in the 89th minute, with Graham Rodger coming on to replace him.

Another 30 minutes to play. John Sillett, who was always confident we'd win because we were such good trainers and were very fit, gave out instructions. "Stand up. Don't sit down and let them see you're tired." Tactically, Lloyd McGrath was told to follow Hoddle everywhere. Challenge and chase for everything. Run 'em around. Gough and Mabbutt were quick on the ground but not great in the air, so get lots of crosses in.

Six minutes into extra time, Lloydy slipped away from Hoddle down the right after Graham Rodger played him in. Lloydy? He's a defensive holding midfielder – what's he doing there? I tried to get into the box as he crossed, but Mabbutt stuck his foot out and the ball looped upwards. Clemence, an England goalkeeper with bags of know-how, couldn't get there. Three–two.

We were in front, but the game wasn't won yet. We knew we had to concentrate, but by this stage we were exhausted. My socks were rolled down and I was playing from memory … those days at West Brom in my teens when Tony Brown and Bryan Robson and co. would yell, "Hold it up, hold it up." Be disciplined and don't waver.

As the minutes squeezed by, Sillett kept urging us on. But the tank was empty. I had scored against Spurs on New Year's Day with 10 seconds to go. This would be some payback if they score now … keep going, keep going.

The final whistle was followed by a moment of silence. I sank to my knees on the halfway line – overcome by feelings of relief, exhaustion and a deep sense of satisfaction.

At that moment you are physically and emotionally drained. The celebrations really began during the lap of honour. You really want to thank those fans who have watched their club through the wind and rain for years when they've never won anything. Now let's all celebrate together.

You wave to your family as you walk up the stairs. Killer is handed the cup and holds it up to the fans, who burst as one into a rapturous cheer. It was a brilliant game contested in the right spirit – Spurs had played their part – but this was our moment.

Chapter Eleven

John was surprised that the dressing-room was so quiet after the game, as we were usually such a noisy bunch and this was the most special of victories. I put that down to the magnitude of what we had just achieved starting to sink in. All of the players were sitting down and looking at their winners' medals in disbelief. Of course we had some champagne in the dressing-room as we showered and got changed. But I also suspect I wasn't the only player having my own quiet moment of contemplation.

Tony Stephens, a very good friend of mine and now a football agent, was commercial manager at Wembley at the time. He came in to see us and we had a chat. He said I was subdued, but I was just reflecting on the past 10 years.

We went up on to the gantry and had a glass of champagne with Jimmy Hill before climbing on to the coach back to the West Midlands. As we were leaving Wembley, I grabbed Micky Gynn and pointed at the scoreboard. "Look at that," I said. It read: Tottenham 2, Coventry City 3 – absolutely fantastic.

The coach took us to Browns Hotel in Rugby – where we worked our way through their champagne supplies. There we also met up with our wives, who'd travelled back on a separate coach. We just partied all night – singing, drinking and dancing – and I eventually crawled into bed at 6am.

The following morning we went to see Brian Borrows, who hadn't played and hadn't even come to the game because he was in hospital. Bugsy, as we called him, joined us on the open-top bus tour around Coventry, which started at midday. We had monumental hangovers, and because the traffic was so heavy it took us four hours to get from the Crest Hotel near junction two of the M6 to the Town Hall.

There must have been 200,000 people on the streets to greet us and the bus moved at a snail's pace because there were so many well-wishers. As the pubs were open, people were throwing beers up to us – and we were drinking them on the coach. Some of the boys had to go and wee in a can on the ground floor of the bus because there wasn't a toilet on it.

In the evening we drank some more, and for the next few days it was just one do after another. Two days later the real party started. The club flew us to Magaluf for a week, all expenses paid and with £500 spending money.

We partied every single day. Get in at 6am, get up at midday, eat, then drink. Our favoured tipple was "la mambas", which was chocolate milk and brandy. Then we'd hit the beach, bars and clubs – and later wander along the street at 5am, find a hot dog stall, get back to the hotel, fall asleep, then do the same thing all over again the following day. We came home for a holiday – for a week we'd been proper Brits abroad.

All that mattered to us was that we were winners. John Sillett has described me as "a colossus" who he'd be "proud to have as a son" and even thinks they ought to put a statue as high as Nelson's Column in the middle of Coventry with me on top. It's a two-way street, though. I owe so much to John for getting my flagging career back on track. My wilderness years could have destroyed me. It could have been the end of my career – and it was quite precarious at times.

But in those three or four years I turned things around and I also found out what Cyrille Regis was all about. You find out much more about yourself when things are tough and you are under fire. That's when you discover if you have fortitude, perseverance, mental strength and character. Have you got determination? Have you got drive? Have you got the winning mentality? Do you really believe in yourself? Can you handle the pressure? Those things come out when you're going through a bad time.

Some people can and some people can't. It was a time when I found out all about myself. What I also discovered was how to play consistently. After 1986 I never had a season when I went through a lean spell. To be consistent, you need to discipline yourself to understand that when you are not quite on form you need to focus on doing the basic things well, so your form will return.

It could have just fizzled away for me. I'd seen it happen to others. John and George came in at the right time for me – otherwise it might all have been so different.

That year I won the Midlands player of the year award, and I also won the last of my England caps. I'd climbed back to a recognizable level again. In short, I rediscovered myself as a player.

CHAPTER TWELVE
Laurie Lamented

With an FA Cup winners' medal under my belt, the football side of my life was going brilliantly. However, the same couldn't be said about my home life.

The Coventry players often spent more time with each other than with our wives and kids, and my home life was declining rapidly. If you are going out drinking and partying and there are girls around, it's almost inevitable. At West Brom and during the years before Coventry's FA Cup triumph I was just the same. In fact, you tend to drink more when things are going badly. It's easy to have a few beers to try to cheer yourself up. Then you see a pretty face, have a few more beers and it turns into another late night.

My marriage wasn't what it should be – it had become a pretence. Even as success came flooding back into my football career, it was ebbing away from my marriage. I was coming home with phone numbers in my pocket and lipstick on my collar and was destroying my marriage big time.

Beverley was a wonderful woman. The fact that everything fell apart was totally and utterly my fault and the direct result of my behaviour. No one can go on having their heart stamped on the way Bev did. She stayed with me because of our two young children, Robert and Michelle, and hoped that I would change my ways. She searched for signs of change in me. For the odd month I would improve, but then I'd slide back into my old ways.

Trust and communication inevitably broke down. We had been together for nine years, since we were both 20. Publicly we probably seemed to be OK, but privately things were awful. Beverley would only come out with me when she really had to, such as on FA Cup final day.

She was a wonderful wife and mother, but I was in a pattern of behaviour that was self-destructive and which I could not control. What makes it worse is that you know it's wrong. You know you are hurting people around you and that you are not spending enough time with your children and your wife. You know the trust and openness you need for a relationship to work is disappearing. All that is obvious – but somehow you still cannot stop the behaviour which causes the hurt and pain.

Ironically, I had shown immense character to turn around my football career – and I was being cited as a football role model, an inspiration to young black players as someone who had broken the mould alongside other black professional players 10 years earlier. At the same time I didn't have the character to change things in my personal life. But I needed to. Desperately.

If you're partying and being one of the boys and not being at home it is selfish behaviour. In my case it was more than that. I was drinking too much and committing adultery. It was destroying my marriage and there could be no justification for hurting my wife. I wasn't stupid. I knew what I was doing and I knew this was wrong. Equally I also knew that I wanted to change.

I was living in two entirely different worlds. Public and private. Professional football can be an innately selfish world. It is all about you, the team, its success and earning the money to fund a good lifestyle.

The club always came first. Regardless of whether one of the kids or Bev was ill, if the club was going on a trip to Tenerife or Bournemouth, you went. You couldn't say my baby is ill, or can I have a day off because there's a problem with my daughter. It would have to be a bereavement or something similar to get excused from whatever the football club wanted you to do.

Many Friday nights were spent in a hotel. And some Christmas Days I would be away in a hotel with my team-mates in preparation for the game on Boxing Day.

This way of life, year in, year out, takes its toll. I went to an England game with some of my former colleagues recently and 90 per cent of the former players there were divorced from their first marriage partner. Playing at the top level can cause real problems for relationships.

All of the things I've done wrong are very difficult for me to admit. I was a football hero, but in other areas of my life I behaved very badly.

It's a horrible way to behave. You have the sporting talent to succeed and delight 200,000 cheering fans, who lined the streets because you have won a trophy for the club they support, but privately you are treating badly someone whose misfortune it has been to fall in love with you and to continue trying to love you.

I loved my wife, but my words and thoughts weren't matched by my actions. Deep down, I knew that the way things were going my marriage was doomed. I also knew that in order to bring about change I would have to change. But something needed to happen to force me to make that change.

Unfortunately, being a dutiful husband – taking the kids swimming or collecting them from school – didn't match the excitement and buzz of going out drinking and socializing. It was too strong a pull. Even though you know there will be consequences. Your home space then becomes a cold place – so you don't want to be there.

I will probably never even fully understand the emotional damage I did to Beverley. And if there is one lingering sadness I have in my life, it is hurting her. She didn't deserve the hurt she felt. She was a great lady – a beautiful, loyal, great mother. She should always have been my number one priority.

The season after the FA Cup triumph, 1987–88, we finished seventh in the league – which for Coventry was in a different stratosphere. We continued to play good football in that second season under John Sillett and George Curtis, but some players had been shocked when at the outset John said: "We're not going to shop in Woolworths any more, we're going to shop at Harrods." Then they bought Scottish striker David Speedie from Chelsea for £750,000 in July 1987.

David was a character. If he was on your side he was a fantastic person, but if you played against him he could be a nightmare. He had difficulties settling in at first and could be a prickly character. When it came to humour, I felt he didn't know where to draw the line between healthy dressing-room banter and rubbing people up the wrong way.

As a striker David was awesome, but for some reason I didn't play particularly well with him up front. Instead, he settled into an attacking midfield role, coming on to the ball when it was laid off. He was a good player – tricky, tenacious and great at jumping in the air to win headers. He was only five foot seven inches tall, and I'm sure many central defenders made the mistake of thinking, when they went up for a cross with him, it's only David Speedie – but he scored lots of goals for us, 35 in 122 games, which is a good strike rate.

David had taken Keith Houchen's place in the side. Despite his incredible form during the 1987 FA Cup run, somehow Keith failed to replicate those performances in the league. In contrast to the four goals he scored in the six FA Cup games in 1987, he got only seven in 54 league games, and he left to join Hibernian in 1989. Dave Bennett was also sold to Sheffield Wednesday in the same year.

Kevin Gallacher joined us from Dundee United for £1 million, initially as a right-winger, then as a striker. We carved out a decent partnership together and bagged quite a few goals between us.

Our biggest disappointment in 1987–88 was relinquishing our hold on the FA Cup by losing to Watford at home in the fourth round. Watford weren't in great form – they were relegated that season – so we'd been hugely fancied to win the tie. So there was no Wembley return for the Cup holders.

The other thing that really hurt was that, following the Heysel Stadium disaster in 1985, English clubs were banned from European competition until 1991–92 – which meant we couldn't play in Europe.

On the positive side, I'd battled my way back into the England squad. And it was even sweeter than getting called up first time around. I had come through a frustrating period of inconsistency and self-doubt. It was a team effort under John and George, but it was very satisfying to be back playing at a level where I was rated good enough to turn out for the national side.

Because Coventry were playing so well, I guess people looked at who their strikers were. It was natural for reporters and commentators to pick me out because of what I had achieved when I was at West Brom, and there were renewed calls for my selection. John Sillett was very proud that he had helped get me back to the top.

I came on for 15 minutes against Turkey in October 1987, in what turned out to be my swansong at international level. I didn't score, even though England won 8–0, but it was a nice little cameo and recognition that I had clawed my way back. Gary Lineker got a hat-trick, John Barnes scored twice, and my old West Brom team-mate Bryan Robson, Peter Beardsley and Neil Webb grabbed the other goals. England were 6–0 up before I got on the pitch.

I hoped that manager Bobby Robson might have been checking me out to see if I was worth taking to the following summer's European Championships in West Germany, but it was not to be. I was a bit disappointed that my performance didn't lead to more caps, but Bobby had a younger generation of players coming through who were at their peak, such as Lineker and Beardsley – playing for Barcelona and Liverpool respectively. Although the likes of Steve Bull, who was still a Third Division player at Wolves, got their chance later on, realistically you had to be playing for one of the very highest clubs to stay in at that level.

In football you get the highs – but invariably they are balanced out by the lows. One day you're playing at Wembley, the next you are at Gander Green Lane, Sutton, Surrey. My nadir came in the FA Cup third round on 7 January 1989. It was possibly the worst day of my career. The result: Sutton United 2, Coventry City 1.

That was a catastrophic moment. All of our preparations had been spot on, as usual. We did the same things we'd always done. We went out and partied, had a few drinks and socialized together. Our form in the First Division had been good – Coventry were sitting third, would you believe, and in confident mood.

It was the first time since becoming a professional footballer that I had returned to playing against a non-League club. I had even played at Gander Green Lane when I was with Hayes.

Sutton had a slightly eccentric and well-spoken manager in Barrie Williams, a poetry-quoting schoolteacher. Rudyard Kipling's famous poem "If" appeared in the programme notes and in all the publicity around the game. If you've seen the comedy film *Mike Bassett: Football Manager* you may recall Ricky Tomlinson stunning the sceptical press boys into silence by reciting the same poem before England's fictional World Cup semi-final.

We should have been warned. Sutton had already accounted for two Football League clubs, Aldershot and Peterborough, in earlier rounds. They were no mugs and, from their point of view, they did everything right. There was no heating in our dressing-room, and the muddy pitch was a great leveller. It was horrible. It brought us down to their level, while they also raised their game.

Tony Rains, whose brother, John, who later went on to manage Sutton for ten years, and Matt Hanlon scored their goals in front of a crowd of 8,000. David Phillips scored for us. Sutton took the lead when Rains, playing left-back, nodded in from a near-post flick three minutes before half-time. We equalized through Phillips seven minutes after the break and then thought we'd go on to win comfortably. But Sutton regained their lead when Hanlon converted a cross from a corner that was taken short – and they had other chances to extend their lead and heap further humiliation on us.

As the clock counted down, we created enough chances to not only draw but win the game handsomely – but we missed a hatful. I had a really good chance but fired inches wide, and Dave Bennett and Steve Sedgley both hit the woodwork in the same move. At the end Sutton were clinging on by their fingernails, but it was their day. They held out.

Defeat at the hands of minnows really hurt. That day the final whistle, despite what I have said about it being the sweetest sound at the Cup Final, was the worst sound ever. It didn't really hit me until I woke up the following day and thought, "Did that really happen?"

To be fair to John Sillett, he didn't lay into us after the game as you might have expected. He realized this was one of those rare moments in football when the apple cart was upset and it was for a range of unusual reasons. "At half-time you tell players the truth, and at full time it's too late," he admitted.

"I can't destroy players after one game when they've got to train for me during the week, then play again on a Saturday. We all just sat together, had a drink and realized it was one of those days."

We quietly got changed and slipped out of Surrey as quickly as possible. Sutton United and Barrie Williams, quite rightly, took all the plaudits. The atmosphere on the team coach on the way back was dreadful. No one said anything. I went out and got drunk that night. You want to blot out the memory, because you're thinking about what the papers are going to say the following day.

Every year when the FA Cup comes around we get reminded of that defeat. It was one of the classic non-League v. First Division cup shocks, like Hereford United beating Newcastle United – the other side of the FA Cup coin.

What did hurt us were comments from the Sutton players who said that we didn't want to win as much as they did. That simply isn't true. On a different day, everything would have gone well for us and we would have won comfortably. Equally, if it had been on a decent pitch and at our ground we probably would have won with ease. It had nothing to do with desire to win.

Look at the next round – Sutton were battered 8–0 at Norwich. Did their players lose because they didn't want it enough? Of course not. They shouldn't have said that about us. We lost because things went against us on the day. They stuck to their task, but nine times out of ten we would have scored the goals we needed to win from the chances we created. We didn't. End of. They had their moment of fame and good luck to them.

Chapter Twelve

In 1988 my good friend Laurie Cunningham collected an FA Cup winners' medal for Wimbledon, who surprisingly beat Liverpool 1–0 in the FA Cup final – TV commentator John Motson memorably described it as "the Crazy Gang versus the Culture Club". Laurie got me a ticket, so I was happy to go along, albeit this time as a·spectator. Twelve months earlier I had been there as a player.

Laurie came on a substitute for Alan Cork for the last 34 minutes, and it was great to see my pal in action again. He had been at Manchester United on loan in 1983 when they reached the FA Cup final – briefly reunited with Big Ron, who really wanted Laurie to play in the final against Brighton. But Laurie had a slight niggle and was honest enough to say he didn't think he was fit enough to play. Most players wouldn't have done so – even though it was the sensible thing for the team.

Laurie had been a nomad for many seasons. He had a short spell on loan at Manchester United, where he played five games after leaving Real Madrid in 1983. He also played for Sporting Gijon and Rayo Vallecano in Spain, Marseille in France, Charleroi in Belgium, and Leicester City and Wimbledon in this country.

He was in his second spell at Vallecano when he was killed in a car crash on 15 July 1989. He was just 33 years old.

Laurie was a truly great player whose contribution to the progress of black players in English football shouldn't be underestimated. In April 1977, he'd become the first black player to wear an England shirt at a senior level when he played in the England Under-21s friendly against Scotland at Bramall Lane, Sheffield, scoring on his debut. That appearance is fondly remembered to this day by the anti-racism campaign Football Unites Racism Divides, based in Sheffield, close to Bramall Lane.

He went on to earn a full England cap in May 1979 while still just about an Albion player, making his debut in a Home International against Wales, and later played six times for his country. But Laurie struggled to settle at one club long enough to put down roots, and he failed to reach the 100-appearance mark at any of the clubs he played for. He was a great player on his day and such a special talent. Like most creative players, however, he was inconsistent, and after suffering a foot injury he lost that burst of pace that made him special.

Managers cherish consistency and reliability and Laurie, bless him, wasn't always like that. He had amazing skills and balance and was truly talented, but you never knew which Laurie you could get from week to week. He was exciting to watch and people wanted to see that all the time. However, you aren't going to get it easily because teams will mark tight and prevent your better players from getting the ball. If Laurie had been able to do these things on a consistent basis he would have been an absolute superstar.

He never really found a home. Perhaps if he had stayed at West Brom for another two years or so he would have learned to be more consistent and disciplined and gone on to be the player he should have been – but we'll never know. I do know that Laurie was frustrated that he couldn't be consistent. He had 11 clubs in his career.

I was devastated when I heard that Laurie had died. We were very close and used to socialize a lot. At West Brom,

Laurie and I would hang out together after training. We used to go shopping or eat and drink together. We were very good mates and that never changed even though he was thousands of miles away. When Laurie was in Spain, Bev and I would go and stay with him, or he would meet us over here.

Laurie and I didn't play golf, as many footballers do. We were just good mates. Laurie was friends with Errol Brown, the lead singer from Hot Chocolate, and we used to meet him in a club called Gullivers in London. Laurie was a smooth operator and always looked good on the dance floor.

We'd talk about football a lot. Often about things we'd try to do on the pitch. Like most men, looking back, most of our conversations were about laddish pursuits. There were no discussions about our feelings, and we didn't open up to each other much about our fears and anxieties, or hopes for the future.

We were two young black guys whose faces were splashed all over the papers. We not only had fame and money, we had time on our side. It was fantastic. When we first came on the scene, some nightclubs wouldn't let us in because we were black, but then they'd realize who we were and we'd get in free. We could get into clubs wearing jeans and get all our mates in too, which back then was often impossible.

No one told us how to handle the adulation we received. No one sat us down and told us how to deal with fame. Of course you are going to get cocky, it is inevitable that you are going to have spring in your step and appear a bit arrogant. We enjoyed our time together, but there is always a downside. Looking back with hindsight as a 52-year-old, our conversations were all on one level – we didn't have many deep personal conversations about our feelings. Most young men don't.

Although I was sad to see him go, I was pleased for Laurie when he went to Real Madrid, one of the biggest clubs in the world. It was rumoured that Laurie had written to Real Madrid asking them to sign him, but I am not sure about that.

Back then, Laurie's future in football seemed so bright. I can just imagine how he felt when he ran out on to the pitch at the magnificent Santiago Bernabeu Stadium for the first time. Although Real weren't enjoying the best spell in their long and glamorous history, many great South American and European players had played in either Spain or Italy, notably at Real, and Laurie knew this was the ultimate move.

Madrid boasted plenty of off-the-field attractions too, including the city's vibrant nightlife. Young people would party all night in sophisticated bars. It was a far cry geographically and culturally from the smoky pubs and clubs of the industrial West Midlands.

Laurie made a seamless transition to life in a new country and turned in some explosive displays for Real, whose fans immediately took him to their hearts. Their nickname for him was "El Negro" – used in an affectionate way for once rather than as a racist tag. While Spanish sports journalists drooled over the innovative and exciting "English Toreador", as they called him, to most of the British press, even though he was playing at one of the most exciting clubs in the world, he was out of sight and out of mind.

In his first season at the club, 1979–80, "Los Blancos" put their miserable recent past behind them by winning the league and cup "double". Their resurgence continued the following year, when Real reached the European Cup final in Paris, only to lose 1–0 to Liverpool thanks to a late strike from Alan Kennedy.

Laurie made the starting line-up for the final, despite having only played 45 minutes of first-team football since sustaining a foot injury the previous November. He worked extremely hard during the recovery period, determined to re-establish himself as the player the Real fans had fallen in love with. However, bad luck would strike again when he was crocked by an ugly challenge in a training match. This delayed his return for another seven months, and his career never fully recovered.

Big Ron, who had followed Laurie's mixed fortunes at Madrid, took him to Man United on a two-month loan deal in 1983. The ability to give defenders a torrid time was still there for all to see, but Laurie had lost his pace. He returned to Spain and his unsatisfactory series of short spells at clubs across Europe began.

We stayed in touch throughout. He was later married for a time to Sylvia, and they had a son called Sergio. Laurie lived in a beautiful house in the Madrid suburbs. But he only used three rooms – the bedroom, kitchen and lounge. There was a swimming pool, but the rest of the house was empty. It's hard to say why Laurie lived like that. He was a bit disorganized, I guess. As long as Laurie had his clothes, could take a shower and play football, he was happy. Laurie was always going to get round to getting things done, but he never did. His house always looked half finished.

I still smile when I remember how long it took him to get ready to go out. He was always saying, "How about this shirt

– or that tie?" He'd take something off, then put something else on, and would spend hours getting dressed – he always liked to look good before going out to party. After a game, no problem, but when he was going out in the evening he'd take ages.

Not many days slip by when I don't think about him. There is talk of a film being made about him, which would be great. Laurie deserves to be remembered for the contribution he made to British football and for the player he was and could have been.

It was so sad that he never got to fulfil his potential. I think most people thought his time at West Brom was just the start and that he would go on to have a fabulous international career. It happened to Bryan Robson, who had a long and successful career with Man United and as England's "Captain Marvel". It should also have happened to Laurie and many others.

But that is football. The game is full of young lads who are amazing players in their teens but out of the game by 20, because they don't have what it takes or don't get the right opportunities and the light fades.

I was driving home from pre-season training at Coventry when I heard that Laurie had died. Apparently he had been to a nightclub – and he'd smashed his car, banging his head, and died on the way to hospital.

When I got that phone call, it triggered poignant memories for me, because of an incident two years earlier when Beverley and I had stayed with Laurie in Madrid. Us lads went out to do a bit of shopping and ended up in a bar. Then another, and another. Eventually, we hit a nightclub. We weren't plastered but we had been drinking all day.

On the way home at 2am, Laurie, who was driving a Renault 5 GTI, a highly tuned little car, momentarily fell asleep at the wheel. The next second we'd hit a barrier and rolled over two or three times before skidding along on the roof. When that happens and you are upside down, hearing the horrible screeching sound of metal against concrete and seeing the sparks – you think there is going to be a massive impact and you're going to be killed. It seemed to go on for ages, and we ended up on the hard shoulder on the other side of the road. If we hadn't had our seat belts on we would have died.

When it was over, we got our bearings, unfastened our seat belts and squeezed out of the car. Then we thumbed a lift part of the way to Laurie's house. Both of us had escaped without a scratch. When we sheepishly told Laurie's girlfriend Nikki and Beverley about what had happened, we got a major telling off – and rightly so.

When I heard Laurie had died I thought of everything he had left behind – money, fame, houses, cars. How can you have all these things and die at such a young age? More questions came flooding in. What is the most important thing to you? What is life all about? What can you take with you? And where do you go, if indeed you go anywhere?

While all these thoughts were swimming around in my head, Laurie's funeral was held in Tottenham. Everybody came, including Big Ron, Brendon Batson and Gordon Taylor from the Professional Footballers' Association, and there was a heavy media presence. Also, there were many people that Laurie had made an impact on during his life and who wanted to pay their respects to this pioneering footballer.

Laurie's death also caused my first – and only – bust-up with Coventry boss John Sillett. Laurie's funeral was at 1.30pm on 2 August 1989. I went to the funeral and did one of the readings, but I didn't go to the cemetery because John wanted me to play in a friendly game at Exeter City that evening.

I couldn't believe it. I thought I'd be given the whole day off on compassionate grounds. Not so. Laurie was my best mate in football – we had been through a unique experience as young black British players together. It was obvious I wanted to pay my final respects. I went to the funeral, then drove down to Devon to play in the friendly. Only I was a little late because of heavy traffic and the time it took to reach Exeter from north-east London, where Laurie's funeral was held.

John didn't even put me on the bench. I was fuming but said nothing. Coventry lost the game after turning in a poor performance. The following day John went through his usual post-match analysis and he started laying into players about letting the club down. Then he pointed at me and said, "And you ..." He then proceeded to have a right go at me. I lost it. It was the first time I ever bounced back at John. I really let him have in front of the lads.

Everyone was taken aback. "Big C's lost it, wow." They could see I was deeply hurt. Later John admitted it was his fault. "I had no feeling for the friendship you had and I should have known better," he said. "It was the only time we ever had a cross word."

I saw John in a slightly different light after that. He came in as a great man manager. But a few other things had happened that he had struggled to cope with.

There had been a similar problem with Lloyd McGrath. This was a tough lad who always put his body on the line for Coventry City – and he was asked to prove his fitness before they would offer him a new contract. It was crazy. Another player, David Phillips, had a row over his contract. There were other small things that had a dripping tap effect. Players began to think: "This isn't Coventry any more." We were all about team spirit, and things were happening that took it away from the way it had been.

A year after his untimely death, Laurie's heartbroken family held a requiem mass in his memory. We told everyone we could think of – family, friends, the football community, the FA – but only his family and a few of his close friends were there. What did that tell you? To me it showed that people move on. Here was this guy who was a role model for a generation of black youngsters, a terrific, creative footballer and a loyal friend, but a year later people had paid their respects but had moved on with their lives.

The questions that I had already started to ponder, such as what if I had died when Laurie and I had crashed the car, continued to float around my mind – and I felt I had to search for answers to those questions.

Where is Laurie now? What would have happened if I had died – where would I be? Is there life after death? Where is God in all of this? Is there really a heaven and a hell? I had fame, money, cars, etc, but these things did not seem that important. It raised the question – what can I take with me?

My search for the answers to those questions would ultimately change my life.

Playing with God on my Side

When my close friend Laurie Cunningham died in a car crash in Spain, there were several pressing issues in my life.

My marriage was on the rocks. That had virtually become clear from the time of Coventry's FA Cup final win in 1987. Our smart house in Streetly seemed cold and there was little communication between us. Beverley wouldn't go out in public with me unless it was really necessary, and any trust that was there had gone.

Deep down, I knew I needed to change, but I was stuck in a vortex of "work hard, play hard" and partying and girls. Even though I was causing Beverley a lot of pain, it was a tough cycle to get out of. I always went back to my old habits – and that made things worse.

Three things helped to change the course of my life: first, Laurie died at the young age of 33. All that talent unfulfilled.

Second, my son Robert was now nine years old and my daughter Michelle was six. Mum was encouraging me to take them to church. In my heart, I always knew there was a God. I just didn't know Him.

Whenever some major incident happened – for example if I had a big row with Beverley before a match – the Catholic boy in me would come out and I would pray. Instead of counting sheep to get off to sleep I used to pray. I would repeat the Lord's Prayer and the Hail Mary for what seemed like hours.

Every so often I would get a call from a newspaper to tell me they were going to run a story saying I was with this lady or that girl – and that would cause me real stress. That happened to me a couple of times during my early days at Coventry. It wasn't the sports journalists I was familiar with, but the news journalists who'd ring me up. I would clutch the phone in terror and think of the embarrassment and shame if my wife, family and the public found out. Again I would pray that my behaviour would not be exposed. Thankfully the journalists in question could never quite make their stories stand up or persuade the ladies in question to kiss and tell.

My mum kept insisting I give my children the kind of strong Christian foundation that she had given me and my brothers and sisters. But the lifestyle I was living was contrary to any message they might pick up on a Sunday morning in church.

The third thing that changed my life was that I knew my marriage was on its last legs – and I wanted to do everything I could to try to save it. I started to attend various churches looking for direction. I also bumped into a friend of mine called Ron Headley, the famous cricketer who played for Worcestershire and the West Indies. His father was George Headley, the West Indies cricket legend, and his son, Dean, would later play for England.

Ron invited me to his church. There one day I met a man called Brian Hewitt, who was the Midlands coordinator for Christians in Sport. Brian asked me if I was a Christian. "No,"

I said, "but I do believe that there is a God." He then said: "Do you mind if I ask someone to come and speak to you?" Months later, I got a call from a man named Colin Day, who was involved with Sutton Coldfield Baptist Church and was heading up the new church in Streetly, and we arranged a date for him to come around to see me.

I told him how I was feeling, and during a four-hour meeting he explained the Gospel to me. He talked about a passage from John 3:16 – "For God loved the world so much that he gave His one and only Son, so that everyone who believes in Him will not perish but have eternal life." Colin told me that Jesus was indeed the Son of God and that He died for the sins of the world, including my sins. I learned that Jesus rose from the dead and is alive, and that He wants a relationship with me.

It blew me away that God loved me so much that He sent His son to die a death that would cancel all of my many sins once I asked for forgiveness; and that when I die, I would be in heaven with Him. All the things I had done, and I could still get a clean slate.

I'm thinking about all the things I've done wrong – all the womanizing, the cheating and the drinking. Could I really be forgiven and have a new start? Is this really possible? I struggled to believe that this could be real, but there was something about what Colin said that just rang true.

Colin asked me if wanted to have a relationship with Jesus. I said, "Yes, I do." Quite frankly, I knew deep down that I needed to change my life and felt that only God could help me to change. I had tried to do it by myself and had failed miserably. Colin helped me to recite a prayer – I remember it to this day. I recall mumbling through this prayer feeling emotional, sad and happy at the same time:

"Lord, I am sorry for all the wrong things that I have done. Thank you for loving me and sending your Son Jesus to die in my place. Please forgive me, I really want to get to know you and have a relationship with you." That was it – a simple short prayer. I felt that I was on the right road.

The following Saturday I played well for Coventry City and scored twice. I drove down to London to a function and went out afterwards with my brother to a nightclub. It was typical of me. I had a few beers and started chatting to this young lady. I ended up back at her place and left at 7am the following morning. I thought: great weekend – I scored in more ways than one. Brilliant.

Then Monday came around I thought: "Cyrille, you're asking God to come into your life on a Thursday, then come the weekend you're out getting drunk and committing adultery." I was so overwhelmed by what I'd done that I was nearly in tears. I used to feel guilty whenever I did it, but this time was different. I was really beating myself up and felt the guilt even more.

Colin Day had left me a little booklet written by Michael Green called *A New Dimension – Discussing the Reality of Faith*. I decided to read it. There was only me and Michelle in the house, so I picked it up.

As I read this booklet it started to make sense. Why Jesus had died for me, how much Jesus loves me, and that my life can change for the better. As I finished the book I was smiling and an overwhelming sense of peace came over me. I had not felt anything like it in my life before. Michelle was in the room with me already, but I felt the presence of another person. I knew without a doubt that Jesus was with me. He was making His presence known to me. I knew He was there with me and that from now, He would always be with me.

It was truly awesome – comparable to nothing else I've ever experienced in my life. This surpassed scoring goals and winning the FA Cup. I can hear you ask, "Are you for real?" Absolutely for real. It was an incredible, life-changing moment.

Michelle came up to me and said, "Why are you smiling, Daddy?" I said, "Jesus is here." Kids being kids, she said "Oh" and ran off to play again.

Oh, I know what you may be thinking. Read the booklet, met with Jesus. How gullible are you, Cyrille? Everything is going to be alright, uh?

All I can tell you is that Jesus is a real person. I know because I have met Him. I have felt His presence and there is nothing like it. I met Him there – and no one can ever convince me differently.

The first thing I did was to call my mum. She said: "You've just made the most important decision of your life – to accept Jesus as your Lord and Saviour."

That was the start of my conversion. After that, I started to go to church more regularly. I was on a high for days and weeks afterwards.

My mother had met Jesus when she was in the depths of despair, sitting on a park bench in the East End of London when our family had been split up – and she never cried about that situation again. She knew things would work out fine. My experience was akin to that.

Chapter Thirteen

There was a strong urge to change my ways and break the habits and patterns of behaviour that were leading to my self-destruction. What I had failed to change on my own, I knew that, with the help of God, I would change.

One of the tough decisions I had to make was to tell my Coventry City team-mates and the public that I had become a born-again Christian and was planning to put my (bad old) ways behind me. Not many players had come forward to say that around that time. Christians in Sport was still a fairly new organization. As far as I remember, only Gavin Peacock and Alan Comfort from the football world had publicly talked about their Christian faith.

This was really tough – and I knew that many of them probably wouldn't believe me. I had always been one of the boys – up for a laugh, pulling birds and drinking a few beers.

I told a few of the boys and, sure enough, I got teased. At the time Kenny Everett was on TV and he had this character with massive fake hands who was a preacher. I turned up for training and Brian Kilcline waved these huge foam hands at me, saying: "Here he is – the preacher." I got a fair bit of ribbing, but I was prepared for that.

When the boys got together for a drink, I would just have one and then shoot off. I had to change my behaviour and was determined not to slip back into my old ways. It was a big challenge and at times I did struggle.

I didn't disassociate myself from my team-mates, I just modified what I did. It was hard, with my mates encouraging me to stay and drink with them, but as I stood my ground, eventually they stopped trying to persuade me. It still didn't feel right, because only people in my inner circle knew. I felt I needed to let the public know about this incredible change in my life.

On the pitch things were going really well – I was playing like I was 21 again even if I was heading towards 32. A Midlands-based journalist who was then with the *Daily Mirror* called one day and asked why I thought I was back to my thrilling best. So I told him. I had become a Christian, my priorities had changed, and I now felt a sense of freedom that liberated me – hence the impact on my performance that day.

As I spoke to the journalist I decided it was time to tell the public about my decision to become a Christian. So I gathered a small group of journalists together and held my own mini press conference.

I told them I had become a Christian and talked about what had led me to making that decision – Laurie's death, the drinking and womanizing, etc. Of course, their natural reaction was to zoom in on the salacious details – wanting me to talk about the women, the booze and other stories. But the resulting coverage a few days later was fair and balanced.

My conversion meant I had to slightly refocus on how I saw things in football. It was less about me and my public image, how I was viewed and putting myself first; much more about my relationship with God and my family, and then football.

Cutting back on drinking also helped. I just didn't like getting drunk any more. By this stage I had stopped drinking too much in the week anyway. When you are younger it is OK – as I got closer to 30 it had become harder to train, so I cut it out. Weekends yes, but not in the week.

However, alcohol wasn't my main weakness. My problem with women and infidelity was more of a challenge.

Colin Day came around to my house once a week and I understood more what living a Christian life was all about. Eventually I took the decision to get baptised.

I was baptised at Kingstanding Baths in Birmingham. During the baptism you are fully submerged in water. This symbolizes that your old life is now firmly in the past and that, as you emerge from the water, you are now a new person with a clean slate and a fresh start.

My characteristics were beginning to change. A new Cyrille with a different mindset, a new set of values based on my faith, was born.

CHAPTER FOURTEEN
Renaissance Man

The late resurgence in my football career continued into the mid 1990s. This was in spite of the fact that Coventry's inspirational manager John Sillett, who'd guided us to FA Cup glory and impressive finishes in Division One, gradually had control taken away from him.

I was still playing very well in 1989–90 and the fans were singing "Cyrille Must Stay" (to the tune of Gary Glitter's "Hello Hello I'm Back Again"). Also Trevor Peake and I had been made coaches at Highfield Road. But when new manager Terry Butcher took over in 1991 he had very different ideas. The former England centre-half came in with his own coaches, Mick Mills and Brian Eastick, and they wanted to get rid of some of the older players like me, Trevor (who went to Luton Town) and Brian Kilcline (who headed north to Newcastle). I went on a free transfer to Coventry's West Midlands rivals Aston Villa, while Butcher bought Robert Rosario from Norwich City for £600,000.

The Sky Blues hadn't offered me a new contract. By now I was 33, and some people may have thought it was time for me to hang up my boots and follow a new route within the game. Even I was thinking that I might have to go down a league or two if I was to carry on. As it turned out, a helping hand came from a familiar face.

A year or so earlier, when Ron Atkinson was managing at Sheffield Wednesday (between 1989 and 1991), he had tried to persuade me to partner Dalian Atkinson, a promising young Shrewsbury-born striker he had signed from Ipswich Town. Now, in the summer of 1991, Ron moved to Aston Villa and I became his first signing. Dalian Atkinson followed Ron from Sheffield Wednesday soon afterwards. I went there on a free transfer and, at the ripe age of 33, earned the biggest wages of my career – £1,000 a week plus a £1,000 appearance bonus. I was also handed a £25,000 signing-on fee.

This was a year before the FA Premier League started, after which players' wages began going through the roof, so although it was good money back then, it was nothing in comparison to the vast sums players would soon be earning in the top flight of English football. Defender Paul McGrath and front man Dean Saunders, who became the club's record signing when he joined from Liverpool in a £2.5 million deal in 1992 – must have been on a lot more.

Ron bought in many new players, including Ugu Ehiogu, Shaun Teale, Steve Staunton, Ray Houghton, Gary Parker and Earl Barrett. Also in the Villa ranks were David Platt, Gordon Cowans, Mark Bosnich, Nigel Spink, Tony Daley, Tony Cascarino and Dwight Yorke – an impressive line-up of talent – and they finished seventh in the 1991–92 season. I scored 11 goals in 39 appearances – not bad for a 33-year-old and almost in line with my average of a goal every three games.

But I didn't play too many times in the 1992–93 season, which was the first season of the Premier League. I managed just one goal in 13 matches as Villa went on to finish runners-up behind Manchester United, who claimed the first of many subsequent Premier League titles. Villa led the table for much of the season, but our challenge faded in the final weeks and we were out of contention three games before the season was over after suffering a shock 1–0 defeat at home to Oldham Athletic. United ended up winning by a ten-point margin.

The Villa side was very similar in quality to that great Albion team in 1978–79, although, if you compared them player by player, I think West Brom would have had a slight edge. Welsh international Saunders, who bagged 16 goals including a spectacular 35-yard strike against Ipswich Town, forged a successful partnership with Dalian Atkinson until he was injured midway through the season. Dwight Yorke took his place in the front line, but unexpectedly the goals dried up and United crossed the line with matches to spare.

By this time I was suffering with an Achilles injury, the Achilles being the tendon that passes behind the ankle. It wouldn't heal, so I had to have what they call an Achilles scrape – sounds lovely, eh? It means that the surgeons cut your foot open to scrape out the grit or scar tissue that gets either side of the tendon, then sew you back together. It's a fairly routine operation, but I developed an infection and it was really sore and tender.

In your early 30s your body starts to change. I had been fortunate enough to have never been off injured for more than a couple of months at a time, so I can only imagine what those guys who go through lengthy spells out of action must feel. Once the tendonitis in my Achilles cleared up, I was ready for action, but I couldn't get back into the side because Villa had an impressive choice of strikers – Dalian Atkinson, Dean Saunders and Dwight Yorke – and they were all considerably younger than me.

No surprises then that at the end of the 1992–93 season Big Ron decided to let me go. I received several offers for me. John Rudge wanted me to join him at Port Vale, and Luton Town, where David Pleat was manager, also came in for me. I even explored the possibility of playing on the Mediterranean island of Cyprus. Instead I broke the hearts of thousands of West Brom fans by joining their arch Black Country rivals Wolves. Graham Turner was the man who bought me, but he soon left. Graham Taylor took over in March 1994 – it was his first job after managing the England side – but he let me go at the end of the 1993–94 campaign.

I didn't get too many starts at Wolves but was on the subs' bench a lot. I was also involved in the club's FA Cup run when we reached the quarter-finals, only to lose 1–0 to eventual finalists Chelsea. BBC 1's *Football Focus* programme ran quite a long feature about me ahead of that game, but I had fallen down the pecking order at Molineux by then and couldn't really claim the cup run was inspired by anything I had done. I hardly played for them – and only scored two goals all season, against Birmingham and Peterborough.

Earlier in the season I came on as a sub against West Brom at The Hawthorns. It was like my Albion debut all over again as I got cheered by both sets of fans. I was flattered by the level of affection shown by the Albion fans. Albion won 3–2, so I was on the losing side, but although you always want to win for the club you are playing for, even if it is against the team you support deep down, on this occasion the result didn't matter to me. It was great to be back at The Hawthorns, and it was a touching moment for me to receive the applause of both sets of fans. After all, they don't tend to agree on many things! It was, at the time, my way of saying goodbye to them and vice versa.

By now I was 36 and had been able to extend my career by looking after myself. But I had so many other things going on in my life that it was often hard to concentrate. In the end, the pitch became a safe haven – a place of comfort. During matches I could simply focus on the football and not have to worry about the problems in my life.

I had become a born-again Christian, which was helping me. I had started to clean up my act, and my crazy days of excessive drinking and womanizing had ended. I was no longer behaving that way, but I still struggled with the temptations.

Off the pitch, my first priority was to save my marriage. I desperately wanted Beverley and me to stay together, but I had put her through so much pain and heartache over the years that it was understandably difficult for her to erase the memories of those troubled times.

For about six or seven months there was inertia. In the end we decided to go to Relate, the relationship support organization, for counselling. It was the best thing to do, because the atmosphere in our Streetly home was beginning to affect our two children, Robert and Michelle. Robert's teacher at school had started to notice a change in him. He was becoming a bit more boisterous – and it was hardly surprising. He would come home from school and notice that his dad was in one room, his mum in another, and that the atmosphere was chilly. Kids pick up on it.

It was while we were attending the sessions at Relate that Beverley told me that she wanted a divorce.

Two thoughts immediately raced through my mind. The first was that I needed to prepare for the worst-case scenario that we would actually get divorced. The second was that my new-found faith was being tested far sooner than I'd expected. I prayed to God, saying I had given him my life and asking him to save my marriage so we could get back together again and return to normality and happiness in due course.

Sadly, for Beverley there was too much past collateral for her to cope with. I knew where I stood, but Bev couldn't make up her mind. When there was a third person there and Bev was pouring out all the things I had done it wasn't nice to listen to. All of it was true, though. Having someone else hear about all the things I had done was difficult for me, but quite rightly I had to listen to it all, because I was in the wrong. It was all the harder for me, however, because I was no longer in the "I don't care" mode – by now I was more caring and sensitive to other people's concerns.

I really wanted to make it up with Bev – with all my heart. Spiritually, it made me think, "Lord, I have come to you to help me sort this thing out, so how come I am getting divorced?" But then I realized that God was asking me to love him unconditionally, not just for the sake of my marriage. God was saying: did you come to me to save you from divorce, or do you love me? I resolved that I loved God. No matter what the outcome might be.

Beverley insisted she wanted a divorce so I, painfully, agreed. There was too much water under the bridge. We then told the kids that we had decided to get a divorce. I then moved out, which was the right thing to do, but I stayed nearby. My mum and dad had tried to instil a strong sense of responsibility into us five kids, so it was important for me to be there for them whenever they needed me. I figured out that living nearby would help.

To prepare myself I'd been reading a book of advice for people going through divorce. It stressed that children don't need material things as much as quality time with both parents, especially the one that has left the family home, and that it was important for me to keep my promises. If you say you will do something, do it. So if I said I was coming around on Sunday, I came around. Living locally made sense. They could visit me whenever they wanted. I didn't want them to be further affected by me being inconsistent and not being around.

I rented a flat within a mile of where they were living. In fact I took Robert and Michelle with me when I went flat-hunting so they would feel comfortable coming to visit me. It was a five-minute walk away, so the kids could come and see me and stay over if they wanted. I always looked forward to that.

The divorce proceedings lasted about 18 months. I wasn't earning the money I once had and I was paying for two properties. I was at Wolves and about to be released and slide down the leagues to play for Wycombe Wanderers and Chester City. All of this happened during the 1994–95 season. In the summer of 1994 I'd been desperate to find a club as I needed an income.

It was one of the toughest times in my life. My long career as a professional footballer was drawing to a close. I was getting divorced and I was trying to deal with all the paperwork for the proceedings. I was also trying to sell the house in Streetly during one of the worst property price crashes in years. We had to get out because I couldn't afford it any more. My earnings just weren't enough, I was paying two sets of bills, and I didn't have enough money to pay for both the flat I was renting and the house. Eventually I sold our lovely four-bedroom home for one-third less than the value I might have expected to have received in better times.

On the football front, the confidence I'd regained during my spells at Coventry and Villa was shattered. I was offered a couple of three-month deals to go to Brighton under Liam Brady or Wigan with Kenny Swain. Surely I was worth more than that? A year earlier I had been playing at Villa when they finished second in the Premier League. The trouble is, once you're in your mid to late 30s people don't know if you've still got it.

I was in a real panic. Two weeks before the season started I didn't have a club – so therefore I didn't have an income. The calls had stopped coming in and I had two homes to maintain.

I kept asking: "Lord, what's going down?" Then I got a call from Alan Parry, the TV commentator. Alan was a director at League One side Wycombe Wanderers, who'd only been promoted to the Football League in 1993. He asked me to speak to Martin O'Neill, the club's up-and-coming manager. I remembered locking horns with Martin on the pitch during my time at West Brom when he was a Nottingham Forest and Norwich City player.

Martin and I met up at Warwick. He was short, sharp and

to the point. It took just seven minutes for him to offer me a one-year contract, which gave me some much-needed finance. Simon Garner, the former Blackburn Rovers and West Brom striker, was also at Adams Park, and we had the oldest striking partnership in all four divisions.

Throughout my time at Wycombe I lived with my sister Nilla in Northolt, Middlesex. Nilla is Jason Roberts's mum. She gave me a room for the season, which helped to ease some of the financial pressure that was weighing heavily on my shoulders.

Jason, who was then 16 or 17, had just been released by Chelsea and was without a club, so I took him with me to Wycombe on trial. He did well and stayed for almost a season but wasn't offered professional terms. I played a whole season under Martin O'Neill. It was good fun – but a stressful time overall. I was playing football and going up to see the kids in Birmingham once a week and every other Sunday, so they would see me twice a week each fortnight. I was also going through divorce proceedings and had to meet up with lawyers and barristers.

It wasn't a messy divorce. We got to a point where the barristers were able to advise us on the best way to deal with things. Everything was totally transparent. It would have been easy to attempt to hide this and that, but I was open and honest about things. One fact that couldn't be avoided was that the best days of my playing career were over.

Chickens came home to roost, all to do with my behaviour. It was painful, but I came through it. I am not asking for sympathy and I am not asking to be forgiven. I am also not expecting people to see me as a role model – I am simply saying this is what happened to me, and I hope that people who read this will see, whatever their own situation, that it is possible to change and become a better person, and that you can battle through life's difficulties to carve out a fresh future.

It hasn't been easy for me but I had a big advantage. I had God on my side. The divorce was finalized and everything was split up and agreed without any further fuss. Payments to support our two children were also arranged.

After my solitary season with Wycombe, I came back to Birmingham, where I stayed with a friend, Dave Barnett, who was then with Birmingham City, while I played for Chester City for a year. Chester, who were in League Two, were managed by the former Welsh international Kevin Ratcliffe.

Kevin realized I couldn't cope with full-time training, so he allowed me to have an easier schedule than the rest of the players. I would play on Saturday, have Sunday and Monday off, train or play on Tuesday, have Wednesday and Thursday off, train on Friday, and so on. I could make an impact on games for an hour or so – then Kevin would bring me off for the last 15 to 20 minutes. I enjoyed my time at the Deva Stadium and played the entire season.

I had gone through the leagues in consecutive seasons – the Premier League with Villa, Championship with Wolves, League One with Wycombe and League Two with Chester.

I was 38 and I enjoyed football for what it was. Fun. The football pitch was my escape from the pressures of everything else going on in my life. When you are young you take all of your emotions on to the pitch, but when you are older you can't wait to get out there, because all of your problems then dissipate.

I tried to take my mind off all the stresses and strains. It was easy to focus on football during matches and training, and it was only on my way home that I'd start thinking about seeing lawyers and sorting out finances. For me football was never work. Well, it is, but it isn't the same as having a job. When you're so passionate about what you do, how can that be work? Exercise has that effect on all kinds of people. It acts as a release.

As I moved down the leagues, motivating myself did become harder. It isn't easy to motivate yourself to play at, say, Scarborough in front of 1,500 people on a freezing cold evening. Especially when you get bumped and bruised and the playing surfaces are poor. That is when you really have to have a hunger for it. I would have played as long as possible regardless of whether I needed the money or not. I love playing football. Not for the money – that's nice, of course – but I love everything about it, including the banter in the dressing-room.

Playing big games when I was in my 30s was never a problem. But by then you have no fears. You have learned to be consistent and how to handle the big occasion. Nothing is a problem psychologically, but physically it is a very different story.

Physically I couldn't quite do the things I wanted to do any more. It could be frustrating at times. Younger players would just skip around you. You had the experience but not the body to put the move you'd planned into action. I had to think harder to outwit defenders. I couldn't explode with pace any more.

After a game it was a bit crazy. My body was broken for

days. The management would let me have days off to recover if I asked for it, because they trusted me to know my own body and what it was capable of. They knew that you were the best judge of when you needed to rest. You still had to do the business for them – but it was about trust and honesty. If they saw you giving your all, putting your body on the line and making an impact on the game, they understood you needed a couple of days off here and there.

At Villa, I roomed with their popular defender Paul McGrath, who was the same. Paul never trained most of the time. He would do some abdominal work or exercise on the bike, or do some shuttle runs and a five-a-side, and he'd still be the best player on the park on Saturdays – a truly awesome player.

When I retired from football, I bought a flat for £42,000 in Boldmere, near Sutton Coldfield. It was close to where my kids were living with their mum, so they could come and visit or stay overnight whenever they wanted.

When the season ended, Chester's chairman Mark Gutterman offered me another year there, which would have taken me to the age of 39 and the milestone of 20 years as a professional footballer. But I had an ankle injury on my right foot and we just could not sort it out. So I just thought it was best to pack it in right away rather than struggle on physically. Finally the moment of retirement had arrived. I was out of the game.

That was horrible. I had never been unemployed, and now I was out of work for eight months. It was a dreadful time – waking up each day without the discipline of work to go to – because it had never happened to me before. I'd been working since I was an apprentice electrician in my mid teens.

Looking back, although I had a long career I feel I only achieved 65 per cent of my potential. If I had shown more commitment and more discipline I could maybe have reached 70 or 80 per cent, and if I had made better career decisions along the way it might have been even higher. It does feel satisfying to have had such a long and varied career, and to have helped to break the mould for black guys alongside Brendon Batson and Laurie Cunningham and others. So, in terms of personal potential, did I get enough out of my career? In hindsight, no, but I am proud of what I did achieve. I was just dissatisfied that I didn't achieve more.

I should have moved from West Brom in 1982, but at the time I had my own reasons for staying. You only realize what you should or shouldn't have done with hindsight – in the thick of things you just follow your instincts. I was in a comfort zone. And to realize your full potential, you have to be out of your comfort zone and continually stretched. Someone else looking in from the outside would have said, "Albion are on the decline – maybe it's time for you to get out." From the inside, you don't see it like that.

It's always best to leave when things are looking up and you're in form. You should never leave when you are out of form and you are playing badly – but that may be out of your hands.

Some of my former colleagues have astute observations on this one. Brendon Batson, whose own career ended prematurely through injury, said: "It takes a lot of determination to sustain a career at the top level, and I've got a lot of admiration for players like Ryan Giggs and Paul Scholes who can keep doing that – you have to sacrifice a lot." That means a lot coming from someone who fully understands the game both as a player and as an administrator.

There has been much talk about what I, Brendon, the much-missed Laurie and others did, but what did we really achieve? At the time I didn't understand what was going on. I was too busy trying to get into the first team at Albion. But with hindsight you get to understand what really happened. And you hear the testimonies of players whose lives changed for the better because of what we achieved and you have to feel proud.

Players like Dwight Yorke, Andy Cole and Ian Wright have all said that we inspired them, and that's very flattering. Young players still come up to me today to say we inspired their dad or they have read about us. That does now make me proud, but at the time, when you're a teenager, you aren't aware of what is happening. You're not thinking: I'm going to leave a legacy, break a glass ceiling and be remembered as one of the pioneering black players who made that possible. Only history has shown that this is what actually happened.

I remember going to a Manchester United game and Andy Cole came into the players' lounge, walked up to me and said: "Cyrille, you're the man." We're good friends now. David James did the same thing. Big Ron even said that among the black players he knew I was "the guv'nor".

The first embryonic thoughts about becoming a football agent stemmed from those sort of conversations. I began to think that if I am held in such high esteem and regarded as a respected figure by players maybe I should attempt to turn it into something positive by offering a valuable service and encouragement to young footballers who are in the same position as I was when I was young and wasn't quite sure how to handle the next steps in my career.

Back to the Baggies ... and Out Again

Most players struggle to know what to do when their playing career ends. The daily routine of getting up each day and heading to training; the need to be physically fit enough to play the game; meeting and playing with your colleagues and doing all the other things that are an essential part of a footballer's life – all these are suddenly taken away.

Without the discipline of training and match-days, the activity, the bonding and the team spirit, plus the buzz and excitement of simply being a professional footballer, there is a huge gap in your life. It is akin to working in an office and the daily interaction you naturally get from going to work and chatting to people. Suddenly, when that is no longer there, you have to manufacture a reason to meet people. The phone has stopped ringing.

If you have been in the limelight and are used to being idolized by fans – or just recognized – adjusting to a post-playing career can be tough. Even if you only play non-League football, you are a somebody in that town. When your career finishes you can feel as if you are a nobody. Some people like the anonymity of being unknown and being able to walk down the street or sit in a restaurant without being approached, but most footballers don't and find it hard to adjust.

The income isn't there either. The public equate fame with money. They think you have loads of money, but even today only some of the players are earning loads. In our day, you didn't earn enough to retire on unless you were a real exception. Cash is still going out at one end. You still have pay all those bills thudding on to the hall carpet every morning. This wasn't a problem when you were working, but it is different when there is nothing coming in at the other end. You might have had sponsored cars and other fringe benefits that you didn't have to consider paying for – now you have to find the funds to buy them.

Footballers are a proud lot, too. Putting on a front is the norm for a lot of guys. We often feel the need to keep up appearances – even if it means living beyond our means once our boots have been laced up for the last time.

Filling the time isn't easy for everyone – going to the pub to drown your sorrows and while away the hours is an easy option for some. George Best and Paul Gascoigne are classic examples of outstanding players who experienced this in the years after they hung up their boots.

The other thing you've been used to is fitness and a healthy lifestyle. Despite some of the drinking I have mentioned in this book, footballers are extremely fit and burn off thousands of calories during training and playing matches. Your body gets used to this level of activity over a number of years. Suddenly it has to cope with a more sedate lifestyle – so it is easy to put on the pounds.

But the main challenge is working out what to do with the rest of your life. Although players leave the game at all ages, few last past their mid-30s – a time in life when most other people's careers are really beginning to take off. Some will aspire to stay in the game as a coach, a manager or in some other capacity. But logic tells you there are thousands of players but only hundreds of coaches and managers – so the opportunities are restricted.

What do you do to get a job? If you have been a footballer for 15 to 20 years, it can be quite daunting to go back into the classroom to learn new skills. Moving to another totally different occupation isn't easy. Coming on to the job market without any background or experience of a particular role is a serious problem. Some employers may feel that taking on a well-known former footballer could be a boost to their business; others will wonder whether your heart will truly be in it. Replacing staff is an expensive and difficult process, so why take on a former footballer who may leave because it's not really what he wanted to do and suddenly someone has offered him a job in football?

After I left Chester City in 1996 I didn't know what my future would hold. I had passed my "B" Grade electrician's apprenticeship with Higgins & Cattle when I was a teenager, but that was almost 20 years ago. Would I still know how to rewire a house?

I fancied staying in the game in some capacity. I had taken a Football Association "A" Licence coaching qualification when I was at Wolves, which meant I was a qualified coach. I'd done some coaching at Coventry City and found I quite liked it. I had also taken a football management course at

Henley College in Coventry, when I was still playing – so I had prepared for it.

The Professional Footballers' Association (PFA) is to be applauded for the work they do to help players get their coaching qualifications – but planning ahead is the real problem.

Doing nothing all day was killing me and I needed someone to give me a break. I was used to the routine – getting up, going to work or training and having a purpose. All of your mates or friends are out working. Suddenly you are trying to fill your day and not knowing quite what to do.

I had applied for a couple of jobs, including the job of manager at Wycombe Wanderers, which John Gregory got, and I was tentatively offered a youth coaching role there which never materialized. I had an interview for the manager's post at Rushden & Diamonds – but nothing happened there either.

I know this might upset some Coventry City fans, but despite winning the FA Cup with them in 1987, the club I am more strongly associated with is West Bromwich Albion. It's true that I played for Coventry for roughly the same length of time, seven seasons, as I did for Albion, but I am sure most Sky Blues fans will understand that I spent my formative years in professional football at The Hawthorns and so Albion was extra special to me.

Albion have always been my club. Football-wise they were my first love. I had some special moments there. It was where I made my name, and I'm sure that if you asked people which club my name is associated with, most would say West Brom. I had a special relationship with the Albion fans too, and always will have. So it is Albion's results I look for first every weekend during the season. Then come Coventry, then Aston Villa.

Albion were my club, and still are, and it was a thrilling moment in February 1997 when my days of walking around the house waiting for the phone to ring ended with me being offered a job back on my old stamping ground. Ray Harford had just been appointed as Albion manager, replacing Alan Buckley, and he wanted me to join the club's coaching team as reserve-team coach alongside my former Albion team-mate John Trewick, who had been appointed as Ray's assistant, and Richard O'Kelly, who was in charge of the youth team. Richard had been a popular player at nearby Walsall.

John had already been on the coaching staff at the club for a few seasons, having worked his way up from community officer, so he knew the club inside out and was a popular and highly respected figure at the club. The long-term plan was for me and John to be groomed for the combined roles of coaching and managing the first team.

I was delighted to be back at Albion and particularly pleased to team up with John again, a former colleague during the Ron Atkinson days, who'd played 96 games for Albion before leaving to join Newcastle in 1980 – which at the time was considered a backward step. John was at St James's Park for four seasons and then enjoyed a golden spell in his career at Oxford United in the mid 1980s, helping them win promotion to the old First Division and capturing a League Cup winners' medal. John's coaching career began in the Midlands at non-League Bromsgrove Rovers under another former Albion midfielder Bobby Hope, who would also join Albion's backroom staff.

Plenty had changed at The Hawthorns in the years I had been away. Albion had been relegated from the First Division in 1986, and they slid into the Third Division five years later, ironically under the management of Bobby Gould, who'd bought me from Albion for Coventry in 1984. Ossie Ardiles brought Albion back up to Division Two in 1993, but they hadn't remotely looked like playing in the top flight – and for many years had been a long way from the new money flooding into the Premier League.

The Hawthorns had also been a manager's graveyard – and that wouldn't get any better in my time there as a coach. Eight managers had been and gone in the 13 years I had been away: Johnny Giles (who had sold me), Ron Saunders, Ron Atkinson (for a brief second spell), Brian Talbot, Bobby Gould, Ossie Ardiles, Keith Burkinshaw and Alan Buckley. Now it was Ray Harford's turn.

Everyone in football knows you cannot build stability on sand – and Albion hadn't had the foundations right for ages. Ray's plan was to bring long-term vision to the club, and I was only too pleased to be part of his new team.

As I was inexperienced in coaching, being reserve-team coach appeared to be an ideal first job, because it was a step between coaching senior players and those making their way through from the youth team. It also didn't carry too much in the way of immediate responsibility. Whatever anyone might say about the reserve-team results and league, the results don't matter as much as the performances and progress of individual players.

However, I soon found that, although it was great to get the experience, as far as developing as a coach was concerned, managing the reserve team was not very helpful – it was probably the worst coaching role you could have. At most clubs you have a first-team squad and a youth-team squad. As reserve-team coach you are working with a balance of players who are in neither squad. Most of the players at the club were training regularly either with the first team or the youth side. In the three years I was at Albion I only ever had about five players to coach on a regular basis.

The players I had to coach were a hybrid group, so I didn't get to work with them every day. The squad I had would usually include a couple of senior players who had been bombed out of the first-team set-up for one reason or another, while other players were only there because they were recovering from injuries or else third-year trainees who were too old to play in the youth team, but hadn't yet made it into the first team.

Consequently, I never had three or four days on the trot in which to develop a squad of players in the way I wanted. You couldn't work on things as a team, which was frustrating. I wasn't benefiting too much in the way of personal development either.

Like other recent Albion managers before him, Ray Harford left within a year, partly because of a row over funds and partly because he found travelling from Hertfordshire each day too tiring. Once again, the long-term plan was re-jigged. Harford's replacement was Denis Smith, who had done well at Oxford United before joining Albion. He brought Malcolm Crosby in with him as his assistant, so John Trewick stepped back to being youth-team coach again alongside Richard O'Kelly. John had been in with a shout for the manager's job, but probably didn't quite have the experience or profile they wanted. It all meant there was no chance for me to step up and to develop as a coach, which I found frustrating.

Denis Smith didn't last long. When he got the sack, John Gorman came in with Brian Little, but that didn't work out either. Brian had lots of issues going on in his private life and didn't do very well at Albion, having previously been successful with Villa and Leicester City.

In came another new manager – this time someone who had more success, who transformed Albion and took them into the Premier League. Gary Megson also benefited from new leadership on the board at Albion and the not inconsiderable funds raised by selling Republic of Ireland international Kevin Kilbane to Sunderland for £2.5 million and Italian midfielder Enzo Maresca to Juventus for £4.3 million.

Gary, who arrived in 2000, was the fourth manager I had worked under in a relatively short space of time and there was a danger of me being a permanent fixture at the club – like a leather sofa plonked in the corner of room. I didn't want to be Cyrille Regis the untouchable popular hero – the nice guy who hasn't got the experience or coaching skills to progress but is good to have around to pacify the fans and because everyone likes him. My personal pride wouldn't allow it. So, after Gary's arrival I thought, it's now or never. I felt the time was right to get out, and I resigned.

Going back to Albion gave me a great insight into coaching and management – but if I am being really honest, aside from any other frustrations, I didn't truly develop the love of coaching that I had hoped. You need to have a real passion for it so you can improve. I just didn't enjoy it enough. Sometimes in life you just have to be honest with yourself to make the right decision, and for me this was one of those times.

At the same time I was mulling over whether to stay at Albion or leave, my nephew Jason Roberts was just about to leave Bristol Rovers, where he had scored 38 goals in 78 appearances. This was a real case of déjà vu. A couple of years earlier at the age of 18, Jason had found himself, like me, at Hayes. He had come to the attention of several Football League clubs and had to decide which one to join.

There were some very different circumstances, though. Unlike me in my youth career (if you can call it that, for no one had spotted me and our family had no background knowledge of the football industry), Jason was blessed with three former footballers as uncles – me, my brother David, who had also risen from non-League football to play for several Football League clubs including Birmingham City, Stoke City and Notts County, and Otis Roberts, a former Grenadian international who played in Hong Kong and Belgium.

I had been able to secure work experience for Jason at Aston Villa and a trial at Wycombe Wanderers, where he earned a scholarship. He had previously been a trainee at Chelsea but hadn't made it there. Like the vast majority of youth players at professional clubs, he was released, and after his time at Wycombe he followed in my footsteps and went to Hayes.

Hayes's manager Terry Brown turned Jason from being a winger into a centre-forward, attracting the attention of clubs like Arsenal, Southampton and Wolves. Jason plumped for Wolves, but he didn't get a look in at Molineux and was immediately loaned out to Torquay United and Bristol City to gain valuable experience. In August 1998 Jason was sold to

Bristol Rovers for £250,000, and over the next two seasons he scored 38 goals. In the summer of 2000, they missed out on promotion.

Jason's career needed managing – and it had got me thinking about the limited advice I had when I'd left Hayes more than 20 years earlier. Fortunately, I had been able to call upon the know-how of their manager Bobby Ross. But that was more by luck than judgement.

Players' agents had mushroomed in football lately – but they didn't have the best of reputations. Most, regardless of the reality of the situation, were painted in the media as money-grabbing leeches. In the 1990s the FA decided to examine the role of agents and set up the so-called "Bungs Inquiry" to look into kickbacks and inducements. It ran for many years but its findings were inconclusive.

The antics of a small number of agents, before the rules were tightened, had left a lot to be desired. Equally, clubs were all too happy to grumble about agents in the press – but then use them to acquire players behind the scenes. Agents were certainly coming into the game more and more.

For me, there was one defining factor that was frequently left out of the equation – the completely uneven balance there had so often been in the past when a teenage boy and his parents sat on one side of the table and an experienced director or manager sat on the other side. Parents and players are dealing with all sorts of emotions and quite often don't fully understand their market worth. Football agents clearly had a part to play, and I began to wonder if I could get into representing players myself, starting with Jason.

I had a friend called David Yelloly at Cadmans Financial

Services, based in Knowle, who I had known for many years. I had told him about my frustrations of working at Albion and that Jason was at Bristol Rovers and doing very well. Back then, if you were a relative of a footballer, you didn't have to have any qualifications or meet any criteria to become an agent but, like all player agents, you did have to put down a £100,000 bond with FIFA. David provided the money and we set up a company called Cadmans Regis.

My first deal was to take Jason Roberts to West Bromwich Albion on 26 July 2000, for a club record £2 million fee. Just as I had been 23 years earlier, Jason was an instant success at The Hawthorns. He scored 15 goals in 34 appearances in the 2000–01 season, forging a successful partnership with fellow striker Lee Hughes, who'd also played at non-League level. Albion almost made it back into the big time, reaching the First Division play-offs, but sadly they lost to Bolton in the semi-finals. A year later they were promoted, although Jason's season was marred by a persistent metatarsal injury which restricted him to just 12 league appearances, in which he scored seven goals.

Cadmans Regis was embryonic and we had the same problems of building up any new business – I needed clients and contacts. Eventually I managed to develop a stock of between 15 and 20 players, but one of the hardest things was getting the relevant phone numbers that you need.

Being an agent has allowed me to pour back my experience into the industry to help other players, in particular through mentoring boys of 16 and 17 and talking to players from every kind of background at differing stages of their career, passing on the experience I picked up in mine to enable them to make better career decisions. It is a job in an industry I understand. If you don't take to management and coaching, what better way to transfer 20 years of knowledge and experience into the game? It suits me down to the ground.

I love negotiating on behalf of my players, ensuring that I get the right deal for them – but that is only a small part of what you do. Part of it is finding a job for, say, an 18-year-old who has just been released by a club. In that case you're almost acting as an employment agency and encouraging them when they feel rejected.

The big advantage I have is my name. When you leave a message people tend to get back to you, because someone will say, "Cyrille Regis called – the ex-England footballer, etc." That does tend to carry more clout than a name they haven't heard of. It doesn't guarantee that you'll sign the player to your agency or that a club will be more interested in signing a player on your books, but it does help to move things along a bit more easily and is useful when you are networking.

I worked as a solo agent for about two-and-a-half years and it was tough. I was always used to working in a team environment, so being a one-man band was difficult. There was no one to bounce ideas off. Also, although I had a small footballer's pension, the income wasn't stable enough, and you always needed to find funds. You also need a decent car when you are racking up 40,000 miles a year, so I joined a big player agency, First Artist, which is based in Wembley and managed by Phil and John Smith. I stayed with First Artist for two years, and then moved to the Stellar Group, representing their Midlands-based players.

Despite what is said about agents, most are decent people.

The only advantage I have is that I have played the game – it doesn't make me a better negotiator, but it does help me understand what a player is going through. One of the things I enjoy about being an agent is sharing the joy of seeing a player making his debut or scoring his first goal, because I can relate to how that feels and what it is like. That is part of the pleasure. My job isn't to tell them what to do on the pitch, it's to advise them off the pitch.

It is easy to forget sometimes the influence you've had on people and the lengths they will go to express their allegiance. I remember being out one day and a man came up to me saying, "Cyrille Regis?" I nodded. He rolled up his sleeve to show me a tattoo of my face he'd had done on his arm. When you realize that someone had been so moved by what you have done that they've chosen to mark their skin indelibly with your image, then you get to understand the impact you have had on their life. You just hope you leave good memories. And that was a good memory. That was somebody, in effect, saying you have given me so many good footballing memories I want to have your face tattooed on my arm.

It's the same with people coming up and saying that they remember me scoring this goal or that goal. The ones I get reminded of the most are the one in the 5–3 West Brom victory over Man United at Old Trafford and my goal of the season against Norwich in 1982. It is a truly humbling experience.

Although I was coaching young footballers and developing my own career as a football agent advising young players on the best steps to take for the future, my relationship with my own two children wasn't always what it should have been.

One of my biggest regrets was having not always had the closest of relationships with my own son, Robert, when I was playing. Those early years are so important in childhood. When Robert was growing up I didn't put enough time into finding out what was going on in his heart. After I became a Christian and I looked back over the previous years, I realized I hadn't been there for Robert and Michelle anywhere near as much as I should have. I knew I had to make up for that time.

I also realized that, like it or not, as the child of a famous dad and a famous footballer in particular, Robert was always going to have to live up to his dad's name and be compared to me as far as football was concerned.

Although Robert liked football, he didn't love the game enough. There's a huge difference. My brother David was also compared to me – particularly as he played in the same position as a striker. David didn't turn professional until he was 27 years old. Although I was probably an inspiration to him, I'm sure there were many, many times when people said: "He's alright, but he's not as good as his brother." That's a massive burden to bear, but David was persistent and made it as a professional player in his own right.

David played for many non-League clubs including Dunstable, Barnet, Fisher and Windsor & Eton before he became a professional at Notts County. He went on to join other clubs including Plymouth Argyle, Stoke City, Birmingham City, Southend United, Leyton Orient, Lincoln City and Scunthorpe United in a long and enjoyable career. He had to put up with all those comparisons. So too has Jason Roberts.

My son Robert had to put up with it in a more direct

way. It started in the playground at the school he attended in Sutton Coldfield. He was having problems around the time of my divorce from Beverley. We didn't feel that the teachers were supporting him in the right way. There was an area near the school which had well-known problems with racism – and there had been incidents where some children had tried to intimidate my son on the bus he took to school. This vicious behaviour, mixed with the atmosphere at home and the divorce proceedings, meant he was having problems.

We decided to take Robert out of that school in his last year. He moved to a school in Nottingham and lived with my brother David for a year. I would drop him off and pick him up each weekend, which was really hard for him, but we felt it would help him concentrate on his schoolwork.

Not long after I had set up as an agent, Beverley decided she wanted to start a new life in Canada, and Robert went with her. Michelle came to live with me and stayed with me for a couple of years. It was great being able to spend lots of quality time with Michelle, and we grew very close. Those couple of years were like a gift to me and I thank God for the opportunity that I had to build a deeper relationship with my daughter – we are still very close today.

Robert didn't settle in Canada. He came back to England after a few months and moved in with me too. Soon I had gone from living on my own to having Michelle with me, then Robert, and then, after 26 March 2002, the first of my grandchildren, when beautiful Jayda was born. But I wan't complaining. God had answered my prayer and allowed me to spend intimate time with my children that I thought I'd lost. It was a tight squeeze for us, but we managed. It now gives me great joy when I listen to Robert and Michelle reminiscing about the good times they had when they lived with me. Now, even Jayda has started recalling memories of her formative years in my home. A great turnaround – I felt that although I had let my children down at times in the past I had been given a second chance, one that I grabbed hold of with both hands. I'm so glad I did. My relationship with both Robert and Michelle is now stronger and deeper than ever.

All this and trying to run a players' agency from home! Eventually, the house became quieter. Michelle moved out in 2003, and Robert went to live with my nephew Jason Roberts for a year when he was playing for West Brom.

By this time I was working at First Artist but still owed money to the bank. Being a football agent, contrary to the popular stereotypical image of agents, didn't mean I was rolling in money. Although I had my pension and bought my own house, I still had to find money to live on and to look after my son, daughter and grandchild.

It meant having to cash in some policies, but I have continued to support my children. Robert moved to the USA and is flying now. He is finishing off a psychology degree and has just started his own retail business selling T-shirts. He is married to a beautiful woman called Saidee and they have given me my first grandson, Riley. I bought Riley a West Brom kit for Christmas and he loved it. They visited last Christmas and it was great to see Robert so settled and happy.

Michelle is now at university studying business. She has a very good eye for fashion and intends to also work in the fashion industry – a joint sister and brother venture in the offing maybe?

Meanwhile Michelle has two absolutely gorgeous daughters. In 2007, when Jayda was five, Renée was born on 29 September. By this time I had remarried and I was with my new wife, Julia, in Ethiopia paying a visit to schemes being developed by the charity, WaterAid. We couldn't wait to get back to see her – she is so beautiful, and with a great character that just has us rolling around with laughter most of the time. I am very proud of Michelle too. She is a great mother to her girls. I watch her juggling being a mum and studying and I admire her greatly. I know that she will succeed at anything she puts her mind to.

It has been great to be able to support my children. I have had to deny myself material things to do it, but that's fine by me. Being able to support my children and grandchildren is a priority for us. They enrich our lives greatly.

My faith was growing stronger and stronger – I was still going to Streetly Baptist Church and sharing my story of how I came to know Jesus with different groups whilst developing and growing as a Christian. As my faith grew, I could see that some of my old habits were disappearing and I was becoming a new person, the type of man that could be a great husband, father and role model.

When you become a Christian it does often take time to develop the kind of character and behaviour that you want – we still have issues from our past to deal with. You may not change overnight but I can tell you this: with God's help you can. There may be people in your life who consistently try to remind you of who you were. If you listen to those people, you will never become the man or woman you are meant to be and want to be. The great thing about living with God in your life is that once he has forgiven you, you are truly forgiven for every wrong thing you did in the past.

People who constantly talk about what you did a year ago, or five, ten, 15 or 20 years ago, only have the power to hurt you if you still believe you are that old person. Actually, it will hurt them more than it hurts you: living in the past means you can't fully live in the present and focus on the future. As I have grown in God, I have had to keep reminding myself that I am a new person and that only God is my judge. My past is now my past, and I am indeed a new person and doing my very best to live a life that is pleasing to God.

The question people have asked me most frequently is why does a prominent former footballer want to become a Christian? They presume that fame and money are enough to make you happy. To me, this is a pertinent question and I feel it is important to let people know my story, so they will know that I have messed up, failed at times and let people down, but even more important to reassure them that there is forgiveness for all and always a second and third chance with God.

As I travel the world and share my story, I meet many people who tell me how inspiring and encouraging it is to know that someone like me, who they have admired on the football field, can get so low in his personal life and yet through God's grace turn his life around.

It wasn't always easy to become that new person, and I did often err. That's where I learned about the mercy and grace of God; and His faithfulness to me. I found I was able to stop swearing just like that. Overnight. That was no problem. It was the same with alcohol – I don't get drunk any more.

When I decided to write this book, I knew there would be one subject I would have to address. It was an incident that I wasn't directly involved in – but would somehow have to take a view on. It happened on the evening of 21 April 2004. Ron Atkinson, my former manager at West Brom and Aston Villa, resigned from ITV after he made a racist remark live on air. At the end of a Champions League game Ron, thinking his microphone was switched off, described Chelsea's black defender Marcel Desailly as a "lazy thick nigger".

Although the UK transmission of the match had ended, Ron's comment was broadcast in several countries across the Middle East and sparked a huge controversy. He was immediately forced to resign and subsequently lost his weekly column in the *Guardian*. A repeat of a Radio Four documentary about the Three Degrees, produced by my co-author Chris Green and narrated by Garth Crooks, due for transmission the following week, was also hastily postponed because it included comments from Ron.

I was staggered. I knew Ron could fly close to the wind when it comes to jokes, but this was something different. In all the years I had known Ron I had never heard him use that particular word.

In defending Ron, some people said: "Well, black guys call each other nigger all the time – what's the issue?" Personally, I feel the use of the word by anyone in any context is degrading and offensive, and I was shocked at what Ron had said. Do I think the words were racist? Yes. Do I think Ron is a racist? No.

How can that be, I can hear some of you asking, if you agree what he said was racist? It's very simple. I was totally shocked by Ron's comment because I had seen at first hand Ron's treatment of black players over the years. I can say without the slightest hesitation that Ron was brilliant with us as black players. He used to speak to Carlton Palmer every day of the week, and Ron and Dalian Atkinson had a close, almost father-son, relationship. They'd shout at each other, and then minutes later they'd be the best of buddies.

While I was at Villa there was one game at Everton during the 1991–92 season when Ron fielded nine black players. The only white guys in the starting line-up were Shaun Teale and Mark Bosnich. In fact, there was a loathsome black-and-white photo doing the rounds which had the caption "Aston Nigger".

He also showed sympathy towards players in trouble. When Paul McGrath was going through his injury and drink problems, Big Ron bent over backwards to look after him. Some might say he liked people who were good footballers and had a bit of attitude about them – and he liked that cool to rub off on his own image. Maybe, maybe not.

After the TV incident some black players wasted no time in laying into Big Ron. Don't get me wrong, I could understand their anger and disappointment – even disillusion. Some of these guys had been influenced by the story of me, Laurie and Brendon, and here was our manager supposedly revealed in his true colours.

But if you put all these things together you have to say that clearly Ron isn't racist. If he was, he wouldn't have had black guys in his team. I think Ron was frustrated with Desailly because the player had made a costly mistake and had let it get on top of him.

Regardless of how you interpret it, I hold to the principle of letting he who is without sin cast the first stone. Many of us say things that, if heard by the general public, would land us in a lot of trouble. I personally have balanced that comment against the many words of encouragement and belief in me and other players that I have heard from Ron.

Knowing the full history of Big Ron and how he has treated players, I am not going to hold him to account for the rest of his life over one moment that we are all struggling to explain. People ask if Ron himself has tried to explain what he said. I have never really had a deep conversation with Ron about it. My understanding is that he cannot explain it himself and has never tried to defend anything he said. It was wrong, and Ron knows it was wrong.

I watched the *Wife Swap* programme on Channel 4 that he did with Olympic gold medallist Tessa Sanderson, and right at the end I saw etched in his face the acceptance that whatever he does he will always be remembered for that one comment. Ron has paid a big price. But then, where the media are concerned he knows the nature of the beast and that he made a massive mistake.

There is also an ongoing fascination about Ron. If I do a question and answer session people will always ask: "What is Big Ron really like?" He is a big character – larger than life, an entertainer, a football purist and a great football personality. That one comment has marred his many achievements in football.

If I speak to people who know nothing about football and Ron's name is mentioned it is always in the context of "Didn't he say the 'n' word on TV?" That is such a shame –

because they should be talking about what a fantastic football manager he was and the immense contribution he made to English football.

I had known him for 26 years. I played for him, drank with him, had laughs and great times with him. I have celebrated success with him, been in cars and nightclubs with him. He slips up once. Am I supposed to lock away the memories of all those good times because of that? With the many mistakes I have made in my life, I am the last person to judge him.

We had a lot of good times together that will far outweigh that one foolish moment.

CHAPTER SIXTEEN
Away at the Palace

When people ask me what I am doing these days it often seems a bit too easy to describe myself as a football agent. Although that is my job, it's inevitably not the side of me that appears in newspapers or magazines on TV or radio.

I have always been willing to give my name and time to good causes, help influence any activities that will benefit others, or raise money and awareness, whether it is for hospitals, schools, churches, sport, children or the environment. Giving my time and turning up at charitable events costs very little but does a lot of good. I enjoy giving back, it is rewarding and, most importantly, it helps organizations raise money and deliver sterling work to people that are at some kind of disadvantage. I am happy to sign autographs, or on the odd occasion to go into a hospital to visit someone to whom I am a football hero. No problem. It is an honour to be asked in the first place.

To me it is part of the social dynamics of life. It is a shallow life if your emotional tank is empty and if you haven't got deep, loving relationships. There are plenty of lonely people who don't have open and loving relationships. What is the point of making millions of pounds if you've got no one to share it with? People say money is the root of all evil. But money itself is not the problem. It is the love of money that can cause so much distress. It's lying, cheating and putting money first and people second that is wrong.

I enjoy raising a few thousand pounds here and there by playing matches for West Bromwich Albion All Stars, even though it gets harder to recover after matches these days. I also love doing a wide range of things in sport like being an ambassador for England's 2018 World Cup bid.

I don't do the work in order to be recognized for it, but it's still nice when that happens. In 2001 I was awarded an honorary fellowship by the University of Wolverhampton. In 2004 I was voted West Bromwich Albion's all-time cult hero in a BBC Sport poll, gaining 65 per cent of the vote, and I was named one of West Brom's 16 greatest players, in a poll organized as part of the club's 125th anniversary celebrations.

A few years ago, a gala dinner was held in my honour at the Birmingham Metropole Hotel because in the course of my career I played for four West Midlands clubs. It was organized by the former West Brom commercial manager Tom Cardall. It was a great night and we managed to raise around £7,000 – which we gave to the clubs to distribute to good causes of their choice.

I am also president of a junior football league run by non-League clubs in the Midlands called the Midland Junior Premier Football League, which was launched in 2004. I was asked to get on board from the start and was delighted to give my time to a competition which supports good quality football for players aged between 12 and 18. Many of the players have more talent than those who play in local junior Sunday leagues, but they are not quite good enough to be part of the academy system. It fills the gap between the two.

By playing for local non-League clubs, and only playing fixtures against other sides in their age group across the Midlands, the boys are benefiting from a good standard of football without having to travel the enormous distances that boys as young as nine years of age are covering to compete for professional club academies and centres of excellence all over the country.

The league, which has expanded from just seven clubs and 20 teams in 2004 to more than 40 clubs fielding over 100 teams today, acts as a safety net for those boys who have been released by the academies. Without it, they could find the move down to local junior football too big a drop, in addition to the disappointment of being released. It is a fantastic league and I will continue to support it.

One of the most memorable experiences of my life was being asked, with my wife Julia in 2007, to visit projects developed by the charity WaterAid in the East African country of Ethiopia. An international non-governmental organization, founded by the UK water industry in 1981, WaterAid works in Africa, Asia and the Pacific region and campaigns worldwide. Its aim is to transform lives in the world's poorest communities by improving access to safe water, hygiene and sanitation. Only 22 per cent of Ethiopia has a water supply, a problem made worse by periodic droughts and famines.

Julia came along with me for the six-day trip. Stepping off the plane at Ethiopia's capital, Addis Ababa, evoked memories of the Caribbean with its lush green trees. We travelled to the

Hitosa district, which is the site of one of WaterAid's most successful projects in the country, the Hitosa gravity scheme. The largest water supply project in Ethiopia, it has benefited 60,000 people in 31 communities, who now all have safe, clean water close to their homes.

Water from two springs was tapped to run downhill in pipelines to waterpoints in 31 villages and towns. I was surprised to see that people had to carry a lot of water for long distances, even in urban areas. I like to think I'm a pretty strong bloke, but I'd struggle to carry the amount of water they do every day – having no other choice.

We went to see a couple of Hitosa's waterpoints, where we met children and spoke to women at the pumps. One woman said she used to go and collect water at 4am and come back four hours later at 8am. She told us how treacherous the journey could be because of the hyenas in the area. If a pregnant woman on her way to collecting water went into labour she would have to make a choice: either turn back or keep on going to collect water. So having a pump in the village was absolutely vital.

The next day we went to Bahir Dar, a city in the northwest of Ethiopia, and visited the Blue Nile Falls, one of the country's most popular tourist attractions. Sixty per cent of the water from the waterfall has been diverted to generate hydro-electric power that serves the surrounding area. I felt privileged to think that I was looking at such a majestic sight.

On the fourth day we visited a place where villagers still use spring water without it being capped or filtered. During the long walk through the mud to the spring, I saw young men washing themselves in the streams. On the way back, we stopped at a village and saw a girl drinking the water. It was really upsetting to see them in the dirty water, drinking it and using it for cleaning and cooking – and then to think of the luxury of hot and cold running water back home.

On the last day we went to one of the poorest areas in Addis Ababa. In the slum, we saw an absolutely filthy latrine – open, rat-infested and located right next to a kitchen. This latrine was used by 100 to 150 people and there was no dignity, especially for women, and no privacy.

WaterAid was supporting a local urban development project and helping to fund the water and sanitation aspects of it, including the building of communal toilets, wash basins and showers. We walked around for two hours and it was fascinating to speak to the people who lived there. But we realized the project was a drop in the ocean in terms of what the real needs are.

That visit really opened my eyes to the struggles people face on a daily basis, and I regularly take part in fund-raising activities and give talks to promote WaterAid's invaluable work.

On a slightly different theme, I am also a trustee of the Jason Roberts Foundation. Jason's a great lad and as his uncle I am so proud of him. He is a shining beacon among today's footballers. When you see some of them hitting the headlines for the wrong reasons and Jason being mentioned in such a positive light it is fantastic. I am still his agent. Like me, he has come from the rough and tumble of the Stonebridge estate – and worked his way up from non-League football to the Premier League.

Otis Roberts, Jason's uncle, started coaching sessions in Stonebridge and is chief executive of the organization. Jason himself, who is quite an emotional person, wants to put things back, both in the UK and in Grenada, where he is quite rightly hailed as a hero for helping – not only by playing football for the national side but also through his fund-raising work and numerous projects he is supporting out there in the Caribbean.

Some things money cannot buy – memories to cherish that are worth their weight in gold. Remember, we Regises go back a long way back with gold. My dad Robert – who was known as Big Russia due to his physical strength – used to dig the stuff out of the hills in the French Guianan rainforests! It was gruelling, back-breaking work – and he can't have imagined that his efforts would eventually lead to one of his sons being honoured by Her Majesty the Queen at Buckingham Palace.

In order to be decorated, you have to be nominated by two people. I was nominated for services to the voluntary sector and football. It seems that some people in the community that I serve realized that I had not been acknowledged in this way for the work that I had done, and my name was put forward in a petition to Buckingham Palace. It was accepted, and I was nominated for an MBE – although all of this was kept secret from me.

When the letter arrived out of the blue in June 2008, I was surprised and shocked. The letter tells you about the award and says you have to decide if you want to accept. I said to Julia, "Look at this." She was delighted and very proud of me.

The reaction in the press both in the Midlands and nationally was awesome. It got a lot of attention, partly because, of the people collecting their awards on that November day, the only ones who were well known to the general public were me and June Brown, who plays Dot Cotton in the BBC soap *EastEnders*. The rest were civil and military people. So all of the TV and radio coverage focused on me and June.

Julia and my sister Nilla came along. Michelle was gutted that she couldn't make it. We all stayed at my sister's house in Acton in West London, which is six miles away from Buckingham Palace. You have to get there at a very precise time – in our case between 10am and 10.20am – otherwise the officials say you won't get in. We left the house at 9am, allowing plenty of time, you'd think.

We were driving down the Bayswater Road, looking forward to my big day, only to find that it was blocked off. There were queues of vehicles for two miles. We tried to stay calm and edged our way there. The silence in the car was tangible as we pondered the possibility of being late and locked out. Why this of all days, I was thinking.

Everyone who knows me knows that I am a stickler for punctuality. It goes back to the lesson my mum taught me and also to my footballing days, when we would be fined for being even a minute late. Eventually we arrived at 10.10am. Just made it. We all breathed a big sigh of relief.

When you arrive at the palace, the officials separate you from your guests. They go one way, you go the other, and then you are briefed by the Serjeant-at-Arms on what exactly is going to happen. It all runs like clockwork, but then I suppose they've done it so many times now!

It was only at that stage that I was told who was going to be presenting my award – the Queen, rather than Prince

Philip. We entered the room in groups of 15. I then walked up to the Queen and bowed. She pinned the medal on my chest and we had a short conversation about what I'd received it for. I mentioned my work for the Jason Roberts Foundation and WaterAid, but kept it short. You're told not to elaborate or attempt to fill the time by asking silly questions like "How are the corgis?"

After about 30 seconds, the Queen shook my hand and gave a slight little push towards me, which is a subtle and elegant way to let you know it's your time to move away and her turn to meet the next person. An onlooker couldn't tell, but it certainly reminds you that when you've had your moment with Her Majesty, it's time to move on.

We came out of the palace and posed for family photos. After some TV and radio interviews, we had a meal at Gary Rhodes's restaurant at the Cumberland Hotel in Marble Arch. We then went on to a private party that Julia had organized for me at a small bar in Covent Garden. Even my nephew Jason made it all the way from Manchester. There were around 30 of us, including brothers, sisters, nephews, nieces and friends. It was a great night, full of family, friends, laughter and celebration, and the champagne flowed all evening. We stayed until midnight, then travelled back to my sister's home for an overnight stop before making our way back to our home in Birmingham.

It was a very special day. I took a moment to thank God for allowing me to have this humbling experience. My life could have turned out so differently, but here I was at one of the most famous places in the world, meeting one of the most famous people in the world.

Chapter Sixteen

I couldn't help thinking how proud my mum and dad would have been to see their son presented with an MBE – and of how, just a few miles west of Buckingham Palace, we had struggled in wretched accommodation when we first came over to England from St Lucia, and how much my parents had to scrimp and save to give us a better life. It was definitely a day to reflect on how much they had achieved and the enormous debt of gratitude I owed to them.

Both had sadly passed away within a short few weeks – my dad of stomach cancer on 12 December 1999 and my mum of a pulmonary embolism on 20 January 2000. I so wished they could have shared my special day. It wouldn't have been achievable without their love and support – and I owed so much of it to them.

When I was inside Buckingham Palace, I had a good look round at all of the paintings and the ornate furniture. This is awesome, I thought, grand, audacious – it made me think about heaven.

All of us one day are guaranteed to leave this earth; I plan to meet my maker in heaven. I stood trying to imagine the splendour of God's heavenly palace. It took my breath away just thinking about it.

CHAPTER SEVENTEEN
A Good Place

Having an MBE hasn't changed my life. In my eyes, the MBE is less about me and more about the people who have enabled me to achieve success in my life – people who have helped me achieve the things I have and played a part, whether great or small, and provided love, help and support throughout my entire life.

Without human interaction and human relationships it is impossible to achieve anything in life. No man or woman is an island or can achieve any one thing purely by themselves. The input of others is always required, which is why it is important to remain humble, with your feet firmly planted on the ground.

I am not saying that because it sounds the right thing to say – or because it makes a good soundbite for this book – but because I genuinely believe it is true. I wouldn't be writing this book without those people who have played a part in shaping the whole man that is Cyrille Regis.

I could not have imagined writing this book at any other stage in my life. I know that I am writing it at a time in my life when I am happy. I am currently in a good place. I am as content as I have ever been and I look to each day with renewed vigour.

Chapter Seventeen

In 2006 I married Julia. She is my perfect partner, my soul-mate. Having one failed marriage behind me, I was concerned that my future wife would be able to accept me and love me for who I am, not the well-known former footballer but simply me, Cyrille, the man.

Incidentally, when a mutual friend called Pam Bowen-Knowles introduced us, Julia had never heard of me. Can you believe it?! Being an avid athletics fan, she had heard of John Regis, but not me, as she had never followed football. To be honest, that was endearing to me.

Again, I thank God for second chances. Julia and I were attending the same church but different services. We were introduced to each other because Julia was the chairwoman of a voluntary organization that was doing some fund-raising. Pam suggested I could help her and introduced us. The rest is history, although there was a long period between meeting and dating and eventually getting married.

I loved the fact that Julia was a successful businesswoman when I met her and continues to go from strength to strength. I'm her biggest fan and just as she encourages me to be all I can be, I do the same for her. She is intelligent, thoughtful and is so giving of her knowledge and experience to others. I love that about her, and I believe I am that way too.

We both love mentoring younger people and sharing our learning curve with others. Like me, Julia has a great grown-up son, called Marshall, who is a talented professional dancer and is doing very well for himself in London.

Julia has played a huge part in making it possible for me to write this book now, because of what she has added to my life. She has never judged me and has accepted me with all my flaws. She always reminds me that I am "a good man, a good husband and a good father".

My confidence had been knocked where relationships were concerned, but alongside my time spent with God, Julia has patiently encouraged me, affirmed me and brought the best out in me. Of course, there are challenging times.

Our mentors and dear friends Kevin and Sandra Thomas always remind us that when two people come together in marriage, especially mature people, it is like a collision occurring as the two worlds join together. But as a committed Christian, I see my wife continuously demonstrating love, gentleness, humility and patience. I do feel incredibly blessed, because not many men who have made the mistakes that I did in the past have the chance to be in such a fulfilling marriage.

So why, you may ask, is it different this time? Clearly, I am a changed man, the past is the past and that is where it stays. But I would say, firstly, we both love God and are 100 per cent committed to working at our marriage. We pray together, study the Bible together and talk a lot. Secondly, I still have weekly "date" nights with my wife to ensure that we spend quality time together.

Our current Pastors, Bishop Melvin and Pastor Yvonne Brooks, gave us a gift in the early days of our marriage that helped considerably. It was a CD set called *The Five Love Languages* by the Christian counsellor Dr Gary Chapman. It suggests that five love languages exist and that every person will have a dominant love language: (1) words of affirmation – when you say how nice your spouse looks or how great the dinner tasted; (2) quality time – which involves doing things together and focusing on one another; (3) gifts – which don't have to be expensive to send a powerful message of love; (4) acts of service – which involve discovering how you can best do something for your spouse; and (5) physical touch – this could be just holding hands or a peck on the cheek. I learned Julia's and Julia learned mine. It really does work and I can recommend it!

Both Julia and I continue to invest in our marriage by talking, spending time together, reading books, going to seminars and having great role models around us to be there if we ever need to benefit from hearing about their experiences.

Looking back over my life, it could all have been so different. There is no doubt in my mind that God has turned my life around. Becoming a born-again Christian has been the single most important thing that has ever happened to me, and it has enabled me to develop an appreciation of the people who have been so crucial within my life. I never think: "Look at me, look at what I have done, aren't I clever?" It is the love, patience and understanding of other people that have helped me get to where I am and to be the man that I am. Without them I doubt you would be reading this book.

There have been so many imponderables throughout my life. What if I hadn't had such marvellous, wonderful, loving parents? I thank my father for having the strength of character to stop panning for gold in the foothills of French Guiana in order to dig out a new life for us in England – and for his hard work, endeavour and pearls of wisdom like "get a trade" – and my mum for providing the unstinting love and support for me and my brothers and sisters.

What would have happened if Tom Dolan hadn't started up Ryder Brent Valley and found us some sponsorship money to kit out our team and provide transport, so we could play matches across North London?

What if John Sullivan hadn't spotted me on Regent's Park on that September morning back in 1975 and invited me to join Molesey? Would I still be an electrician who enjoyed his Sunday morning football?

What if Ian Bath, when he joined Molesey from Hayes, hadn't bothered to call his former club and tip them off about me and urge them to come and have a look at me? Would I have gone elsewhere but not been offered the same opportunities?

What if Bobby Ross hadn't helped me to secure a move into the professional game – in the hope that I might get the chance to enjoy the sort of career he had in football?

What if Ronnie Allen hadn't come to see me play and been prepared to put his money on the line to buy me for West Brom?

What if Murtella Groce (Sis) hadn't shown me warmth and affection and I had been homesick and thought: "I miss my family and friends. I want to go back home to London"? Her love for a stranger had a remarkable impact on my career. What if she had been cold and unwelcoming and cooked awful food?

Sis treated me so well. I love her to bits. She is 95 now and lives in a care home; she needs lots of care now as she has dementia. It is 33 years since we first met and I still go to see her regularly, although it is difficult to visit for long periods as sometimes she remembers me and at other times she doesn't. Sometimes we sing Christian songs together. She was my unconditional second mother and is also godmother to my son, Robert.

Robert came to see Sis with me last Christmas. Afterwards he stepped outside and burst out crying. He used to visit her regularly when he was in England, and seeing her suffering from dementia broke his heart. His memories of her were still vivid, and after the visit we sat and talked about how wonderful Sis was, and how she could cook up a storm.

If you went to see Sis, you would make sure you didn't eat in advance as she would prepare a banquet for you. She'd ask you what you wanted to eat and although you'd usually say a cup of tea or a sandwich would do, she would get the pans out and start rustling up large meals which you simply couldn't refuse, neither would you want to.

Because I didn't eat breakfast when I played at Albion (and still don't), I used to feel guilty when she came up to my room every morning with a huge plateful of sausages, baked beans, fried plantain, fried bread and a cup of tea. "Sis, I don't eat in the morning," I used to say, but she did that for months. Every evening, Sis would lay out enormous meals with separate plates for vegetables, rice and fried chicken, and I would say, "Sis, just put it all on one plate, please." It took her ages to do so, as that was how she had been taught to serve a meal to guests. I love her dearly and will forever be grateful and thankful for having Sis in my life.

What if Big Ron hadn't joined Albion? What if Ron hadn't signed Brendon to join me and Laurie? Would the Three Degrees have been established? Would we have played the great football that we did? Or if Ron hadn't signed me for Aston Villa when it seemed my days in the top flight were over?

What if my West Brom team-mates hadn't urged me to "hold it up" – to keep the ball to order to bring them into the game? What if I hadn't learned by rote those invaluable skills that would enable me to stay in the professional game for so long that one sunny afternoon at Wembley in 1987 I could keep possession and waste vital seconds when my team, Coventry City, was winning an FA Cup final?

What if John Sillett and George Curtis hadn't turned my career around at Coventry City and helped me become an FA Cup winner and get back into the England side? Would the light that burned so brightly in my early career have flickered out? John said they should build a memorial to me in Coventry. Only after they have constructed one to John first, surely?

What if after I spoke to Colin Day he hadn't left that booklet for me to read? If I hadn't decided to seek answers from God and look to make a new life for myself, would I have stayed the way I was and been locked in a selfish mode that would almost certainly have led to a premature end to my career and self-destruction? Who knows where I might have been today?

I am proud to call myself a born-again Christian – and thank endlessly the people who have helped shape my faith.

Since my own day at the palace, in January 2010 we received the fantastic news that Jason Roberts is to become an MBE – awarded, quite rightly, for "service for the community" for the excellent work he has done both in the UK and Grenada. It is wonderful to think that it isn't just me and my brother David who prospered in sport by having long careers in professional football, but also Jason. His sister Yasmine Regis is a notable athlete. She is the UK Under-21 triple jump record holder and is currently on a scholarship in Texas. My brother David's son Daren is an England Under-18 football international. But I am proud of all of my family for their respective achievements.

I have had an amazing life. From being that little boy whose first memory was staring down a dusty dirt track in Maripasoula to being the mature and contented man striding forward to be decorated by Her Majesty the Queen at Buckingham Palace – and all that has been in between. From being the powerful centre-forward who thrilled fans by racing towards goal and letting fly with thunderous shots to being head of the men's department at my local church, New Jerusalem.

When I look back, can I say I influenced people? Ultimately that is for others to judge. I know I gave a lot of pleasure through my football. I am reminded of it almost daily when someone wants to share their recollections of a goal I scored or a match I played in.

Was I a role model? Many players have said I was. Did I do enough to help other people? I hope so.

I have shared my highs and lows with you throughout this book. Some things I am immensely proud of – others far less so. But this book only takes us so far. One's life is never complete. We just move from one phase to another throughout our lives – it is true, life is a journey. In some respects it is strange that footballers are asked to write their life stories when they are still playing or just at the end of their careers. It makes sense in one way (to capitalize on their name while they are in the public mind, obviously), but on the other hand it seems somehow incomplete.

We each of us have our vocations in life and have transitional roles. God gave us all a purpose. Part of mine was to play football. I just hope I did well enough.

My parting words to you are these. Have a vision for your life, set goals and aim high. Life is for living. You may make mistakes or fail, but there is always a lesson that you can learn from those mistakes and failures. Try to learn the lesson quickly and use the experience to grow.

I am living proof that you can succeed in spite of circumstances, your environment, criticism and self-inflicted errors. Surround yourself with people that will encourage you, lift you up and not pull you down.

All of this transformation was possible because I was determined to succeed in football and also in my personal life. Once I decided that success was my only option and began to align my behaviour to my choices, things changed. God was with me through the challenges and moments when I struggled, and He will be there for you too – you've just got to ask Him.

I look back over my life and can say that, although I have some regrets, I have so much to be thankful for and so much that I am proud of.

I am so proud of my wife, our friendship and the life we have together. She completes me. My relationship with my children is the best it has ever been, and they are doing so well in their lives. My grandchildren give me so much joy.

I have had a great career and continue to enjoy a rewarding career in what the great Brazilian footballer Pele described as "the beautiful game". I have the privilege to mentor players, and men in general, sharing the wisdom I have gained through life.

I can truly say – I am in a good place and excited about the next phase of my life.

Cyrille Regis – For the Record

1975–1976: Molesey
40 appearances, 27 goals

1976–1977: Hayes
61 appearances, 24 goals

1977–1984: West Bromwich Albion
297 appearances, 5 sub appearances, 112 goals

Breakdown
League: 233 appearances, 4 sub appearances, 82 goals

FA Cup: 25 appearances, 10 goals

League Cup: 27 appearances, 1 sub appearance, 16 goals

Other: 12 appearances, 4 goals

1984–1991: Coventry City
274 appearances, 62 goals

Breakdown
League: 231 appearances, 6 sub appearances, 47 goals

FA Cup: 15 appearances, 1 sub appearance, 3 goals

League Cup: 24 appearances, 12 goals

Other: 4 appearances

1991–1993: Aston Villa
54 appearances, 9 sub appearances, 12 goals

Breakdown

League: 46 appearances, 6 sub appearances, 12 goals

FA and League Cup: 8 appearances, 3 sub appearances

1993–1994: Wolverhampton Wanderers
10 appearances, 13 sub appearances, 2 goals

Breakdown

League: 8 appearances, 11 sub appearances, 2 goals

FA Cup: 1 appearance, 2 sub appearances

Anglo-Italian Cup: 1 appearance

1994–1995: Wycombe Wanderers
33 appearances, 5 sub appearances, 10 goals

Breakdown

League: 30 appearances, 5 sub appearances, 9 goals

FA and League Cup: 3 appearances, 1 goal

1995–1996: Chester City
33 appearances, 7 goals

Breakdown

League: 29 appearances, 7 goals

FA Cup: 3 appearances

League Cup: 1 appearance

England senior team 1982–1987
5 appearances

Index

Index